"Kimberly Wiefling's d‹   ;s shatters
the myth that the road   'esight and
planning. By dissecting   successful
women, this book demonstrates why the virtues of persistence, impro-
visation, and embracing messiness and unpredictability are hallmarks
of great leaders—and why the ability to develop and stick to a master
plan is an overrated virtue."
Robert I. Sutton, http://bobsutton.typepad.com/, **Stanford Professor and author of** *Good Boss, Bad Boss: How to Be the
Best...and Learn from the Worst*, http://amzn.to/bL1Y6R[1]

"Kimberly Wiefling has created a book that should be required for
women of all ages...regardless of whether they are self-employed or
employees (and, if an employee, regardless of their 'level' within a
company). Each woman featured in this book has achieved significant
career success (based on their own personal definition of 'success')
and never let obstacles deter their journey. During the toughest times,
faced with the biggest challenges, they tapped into their creativity,
gut, and brains, and pushed through. Even as a successful
twenty-year business owner myself, I learned valuable information
from each of their stories and was inspired by all of them."
**Lisa Orrell, CPC, The Promote U Guru, Branding Expert,
Marketing Consultant, Business Coach, Speaker & Author,
PromoteUGuru.com,** http://www.PromoteUGuru.com

"Ever have a day when everything goes wrong and you feel lost,
defeated, and ready to quit? Well that is when you need to pick up this
book and read a chapter. It will energize you with stories of women
who faced tough challenges, and beat the odds on their road to
success. These stories will save your sanity, keep you afloat and
inspire you to pursue your dreams. Keep it handy when you need an
energy boost!"
Mala Devlin, Author of *The Software Soul,* http://amzn.to/96EdtT[2]

---

1. www.amazon.com/Good-Boss-Bad-Best-Learn/dp/0446556084/ref=sr_1_1?
ie=UTF8&s=books&qid=1275129038&sr=8-1
2. www.amazon.com/Software-Soul-Mala-Dev-
lin/dp/0578032651/ref=sr_1_6?ie=UTF8&s=books&qid=1275148162&
sr=8-6

"Scrappy Women in Business *is a terrific shot in the arm of a book for all of us out there building our lives and our careers on the front lines of the 21*st *Century. The book is an empowering combination of the honest, wise, practical and humorous advice and experiences of a dozen remarkable women. Kimberly's own compelling story unfolds through the commentary she uses to weave together the remarkable stories of her eleven high-achieving colleagues. Here are intriguing examples and very practical advice to encourage you to keep on keeping on, scrappily changing the status quo while living up to your own potential and improving the lives and environment all around you. As Kimberly so aptly sums up in her book, 'Wooo hooo!'"*
Leslie Field, Ph.D., Founder and Managing Member of SmallTech Consulting, LLC, http://www.smalltechconsulting.com/, **Founder and CEO of Ice911 Research Corporation,** http://ice911.org/, **Consulting Professor in Electrical Engineering at Stanford University,** http://www.stanford.edu/%7Elafield/

"You've heard of the theory of "Six Degrees of Separation?" In Silicon Valley I haven't yet been able to make it more than three degrees before people are connected to Kimberly Wiefling. Everyone has a story to tell about Kimberley. Everyone who's been in her sphere of influence has been affected in some way. Kimberly doesn't ever sit still and she doesn't allow people around her to sit still either. She constantly goads those of us lucky enough to hang around her into new/better/different ways of doing things. Falling into her web, she instigated me to start the first ever university extension blog, now coming up to 4 years old with more than 30 regular bloggers on the art of project management (http://www.SVProjectManagement.net). For those not lucky enough to know Kimberly, this book is your chance of being inspired into doing the impossible. It will be a book I give my daughter when she graduates from college."
Sandra A. Clark, Director of Communications, UCSC Extension in Silicon Valley, http://www.ucsc-extension.edu/

"Finally, a book about real women who broke the boundaries and are living proof that anything is possible. I've been fortunate enough to know some of these women in person. I am a refugee from Russia who came into the United States about nineteen years ago and today I am a Director of Quality Assurance. Some of you might say, what's the big deal? Well, it is a big deal to me. Nineteen years ago I could not imagine being in a management position. I am living my dream because of the kind of women who wrote this book. They've been a huge inspiration for me, they taught me that everything is possible and no, you don't need to bend or beg, just get scrappier. I don't have any words of wisdom, I just wish after you are done reading this book you will be inspired to live your dream! Check the stats, there are 50% women in management and only a dozen female CEOs of Fortune 500 companies. Well ladies, I guess it is time to beat the odds against us."

Irina Elent, Director of Quality Assurance, Quantivo Corporation

"Having spent decades working to expand the impact that women leaders have in the business world, I'm truly thrilled that these women have chosen to share their unique and sometimes 'untidy' paths to career success. Kimberly's book is an invitation for all of us to engage in authentic sharing of the truth of our own scrappy experiences up the career ladder so that others that come after us will not feel so alone when they take a few tumbles or missteps on the way to achieving their dreams."

Denise Brosseau, CEO, Well-Connected Leader, Inc., http://www.brosseaugroup.com/ and Co-founder Springboard Enterprises, http://www.springboardenterprises.org/ and Invent Your Future, http://www.inventyourfuture.com/

Scrappy Women in Business

Living Proof that Bending the Rules
Isn't Breaking the Law

By Kimberly Wiefling and
11 Scrappy Coauthors

A Happy About® series
20660 Stevens Creek Blvd., Suite 210,
Cupertino, CA 95014

Copyright © 2010 by Scrappy About™

First Printing: July 2010
Paperback ISBN: 978-1-60005-185-2 (1-60005-185-5)
eBook ISBN: 978-1-60005-186-9 (1-60005-186-3)
Place of Publication: Silicon Valley, California, USA
Paperback Library of Congress Number: 2010930090

Trademarks

Warning and Disclaimer

Editor's Note

Welcome to the Scrappy Women in Business™ Sisterhood! Our Scrappy brothers are certainly welcome, too, and if you're the kind of men we enjoy hanging with, you'll be relieved to know that you don't have to smoke a big fat cigar to join or swill more than your body weight in beer. But you might have to bare you soul and show your scars. That's right—no one gets into the Scrappy Businesswomen's Hall of Fame unscathed. (Not that we'd trade the experience for anything in the world!) *Scrappy Women in Business: Living Proof that Bending the Rules Isn't Breaking the Law* is an entertaining and inspiring collection of true stories of women who overcame the negative voices around them—and sometimes within them—to create extraordinary lives. Gracious but determined, these resilient professionals ignored the easy path, didn't take "no" for an answer, and frequently swam against the tide to achieve success.

"Hanging in there" succinctly sums up their collective secret to success. But that's easier said than done. We all need a little help sometimes. If you've ever had "one of those days" when your coworkers seemed to grow horns, or you were tempted to sink into the icy couch of despair, reading these stories will help buoy your spirits and realize that you're not alone. Just one chapter from this book will inspire and energize you for the next sprint. If you're a seasoned professional, you'll see some of your own journey reflected in these stories. And if you're just starting out, the wisdom in this guide will save you a whole lot of time and aggravation.

While these women's stories are remarkable, I'm sure that each of you has your own unique story to share. You're invited to share your own story at http://www.ScrappyWomen.biz, a website which grew out of this Scrappy gal-pal project. This collaborative website will grow this collection of stories from a trickle of wisdom into a fountain of inspiration from which we sincerely hope millions of women will drink. Our collective voices will ultimately build a supportive platform from which women everywhere will gain the courage to leap boldly into their own remarkable futures. Visit and add your stories to ours so that, drop by drop, we can grow this tiny stream into an ocean of wisdom.

Keep it Scrappy!

- Kimberly

Meet the Scrappy Guides™

The Scrappy Guides™ are books to help you be unrealistic and accomplish what seems impossible, but is merely difficult. Those of you who say it can't be done should stay out of the way of those of us doing it!

Scrappy means ATTITUDE.

Scrappy means not relying on a title to be a leader.

Scrappy means being willing to take risks and put yourself out there.

Scrappy means doing the right thing, even when you don't feel like it.

Scrappy means having the steely resolve of a street fighter.

Scrappy means sticking to your guns even if you're shaking in your boots.

Scrappy means being committed beyond reason to making a difference.

Scrappy means caring about something more than you care about being comfortable, socially acceptable, or politically correct.

Scrappy means being absolutely, totally committed to extraordinary results.

Scrappy means EDGY!...and is your edge in achieving outrageous results even when they seem impossible.

The Scrappy Guides™ help you muster the courage and commitment to pursue your goals—even when there is no evidence that you can succeed—yet! They are your shield against the naysayers who will try to undermine you, and they will give you comfort during the inevitable setbacks that accompany most worthy pursuits. When you fail, fail fast, fail forward, in the direction of your goals, lurching fitfully if you must. Sometimes success is built on the foundation of a very tall junk pile.

Let's get Scrappy!

The Books in the Scrappy Guides™ Series

Kimberly Wiefling
Scrappy Project Management: The 12 Predictable and Avoidable Pitfalls Every Project Faces

Julie Abrams, Carole Amos, Eldette Davie, Mai-Huong Le, Hannah Kain, Sue Lebeck, Terrie Mui, Pat Obuchowski, Yuko Shibata, Nathalie Udo, Betty Jo Waxman, Kimberly Wiefling
Scrappy Women in Business: Living Proof That Bending the Rules Isn't Breaking the Law

Michael Seese
Scrappy Information Security: The Easy Way to Keep the Cyber Wolves at Bay
Scrappy Business Contingency Planning: How to Bullet-Proof Your Business and Laugh at Volcanoes, Tornadoes, Locust Plagues, and Hard Drive Crashes

Michael Horton
Scrappy General Management: Common Sense Practices to Avoid Calamities, Catastrophes, and Lackluster Results for Corporations and Small Businesses

Meet the Scrappy Guides^{TM} Executive Editor

Hi, I'm Kimberly Wiefling, Founder and President of my own consulting business, Wiefling Consulting, Executive Editor of the Scrappy Guides^{TM}, and the Author of *Scrappy Project Management: The 12 Predictable and Avoidable Pitfalls Every Project Faces*, growing in popularity around the world and published in Japanese by Nikkei Business Press. The biggest compliment that anyone has ever paid me is that I am a "force of nature." Actually, I'm not sure they meant it in a positive way—they certainly could have been referring to destructive forces like hurricanes, tsunamis, earthquakes, and the like. Nevertheless, Mother Nature is one of my favorite gal pals, and I'm pleased to be associated with her in this way.

My dad was a welder, my brothers were both welders, and, if I had been born a boy, I probably would have been a welder, too! But, as luck would have it, I grew up in a time when girls weren't encouraged to be welders. So I went to college instead, earning a B.S. in chemistry and physics and an M.S. in physics. But don't be so quick to write me off, 'cause I've got marketable skills, too! For example, I earned a marksman's ribbon while in the U.S. Air Force right after high school (I used my GI Bill money to pay for college), where I learned to repair electronics equipment. And I spent ten years working at HP in various engineering and technical jobs, including one that involved a long stretch of explosion testing and other destructive testing of lovingly handcrafted one-of-a-kind R&D prototypes. (My motto was, "When it absolutely, positively has to be destroyed overnight—bring it to me!") I got bored with all of the stability and job security of HP, so I quit and joined a series of failed startups (not all my fault!) and then started my own consulting company during the dot-com bust of 2001—not exactly the most hospitable environment in which to launch a business. I lurched fitfully forward for three long years before my big break came—a chance to work in Japan with my Japanese "sister" Yuko Shibata of ALC Education, Inc. starting up their Global Management Consulting Group.

In typical Silicon Valley style, I've helped to start, run, and grow about a dozen small businesses, some of which are still in business and profitable. My clients include Cisco Systems, Symantec, Intuit, HP, Agilent Technologies, Mazda, Daiichi Sankyo, Dow Corning Toray, Mitsubishi Heavy Industries, the University of California, Siemens, Hitachi, Alcoa, Xerox PARC, NECsoft, NTT DoCoMo, and many more.

Now I do more than half of my consulting work in Japan, traveling there every month with a team of people who deliver intensive workshops that enable participants to achieve what seems impossible but is merely difficult. (That's my specialty!) These global leaders emerge from these programs with new eyes to see the opportunities in which we are all swimming, a global mindset, and the determination to solve global problems profitably—for their companies and for the sake of all the people of the world. It's like a dream come true for me, and my experiences have ranged from hilarious to deeply moving.

In pursuit of planetary transformation, I'm contributing to making the world a better place in a number of ways. I'm the Co-founder of the Open Kilowatt Institute (OKI) and the Founding Co-chair of the SDForum Engineering Leadership Special Interest Group (EL SIG). I'm supporting micro-finance for entrepreneurs throughout the world via Kiva, and I support the economic independence of women in various ways because I believe that this is the most effective way raise the quality of life for all people.

I am obsessed with collaboration, and you can reach me via email at kimberly@wiefling.com.

Praise for Kimberly Wiefling's Work

"Kimberly Wiefling has a passion for doing what seems impossible—she not only inspires but actually opens your thinking so that you can ignite your own passion—both professional and personal. She is a master at taking those possibilities and designing amazing, and at the same time, reliable pathways for extraordinary success. As a wonderful plus, she is one of the most entertaining leaders, speakers and facilitators that I have ever encountered in the business world."
Barbara Fittipaldi, President and CEO, Center for New Futures,
http://www.centerfornewfutures.com/

"To put it simply, I would never bet against Kimberly—failure is just not in her vocabulary. I have great admiration and respect for her ability to guide individuals, teams and projects to success. As a colleague, and in many ways a student, of hers, she quickly demonstrated to me how to achieve your goals regardless of your background and experience."
Jateen Parekh, Co-Founder, CTO, COO, Jelli, Inc.,
http://www.jelli.com/

Become a Scrappy Guides™ Author

Have a Scrappy streak in you? Want to write about it? Contact me and let's talk! Email me at kimberly@wiefling.com.

Contribute Your Story to the ScrappyWomen.Biz Website

Want to share your own story as a Scrappy Woman in Business? Visit http://www.ScrappyWomen.biz and submit your Scrappy story of hope and inspiration for consideration. It's easy! And as long as it's not smutty, mean-spirited, or hateful, we'll probably publish it. (Naturally you have to sign a release, blah, blah, blah. Legal stuff.)

Visit the www.ScrappyWomen.Biz Website for Special Offers

Special offers, such as volume discounts, package deals that combine books, coaching and workshops, and guidance on how to bring Scrappy Women in Business events into your company or organization, are available at http://www.ScrappyWomen.biz.

Invite a Scrappy Businesswoman Into Your World

Many of our authors are gifted coaches, lively speakers, and experienced workshop facilitators. If you're moved by the stories in this book, consider inviting one or more of our Scrappy Businesswomen to get personally involved in your community. Contact Kimberly Wiefling at kimberly@wiefling.com and ask for the Scrappy Inner Circle Discount.

Dedication

This book is dedicated to every woman who's ever broken through a barrier, violated a taboo, or overcome seemingly insurmountable obstacles to achieve what seemed impossible, but was merely difficult ...without even breaking a nail, or whining about it if she did.

Acknowledgments

Late one night when there was nothing good on TV, I got this idea to collect the stories of some of the Scrappiest businesswomen I know and admire into a book. "How hard could that be?" I thought. Well, buddy, let me tell you, there's nothing easy about getting twelve vibrant, strong-willed women to agree on anything! But, thanks to the commitment of these authors to sharing their wisdom and experience, this book—which began as a dream—has come to life. I'm deeply grateful for their generous contributions to this book, which took many hours out of their already overly busy lives. And I'm especially thankful for their willingness to openly discuss many personal details of their amazing journeys. As I read each chapter I felt genuinely honored to be able to glimpse some of what made them into the amazing women I admire today. Their stories are the heart and soul of this book, and I merely stitched them together, as if I were assembling a beautiful quilt from the most extraordinary patches.

Having been entrusted with their precious stories, at one point I started to despair that I wouldn't be able to do them justice with my editing skills. After all, the success of my first book, *Scrappy Project Management*, might have just been a fluke! Then it hit me—I had a secret weapon when I wrote that book—DeAnna Burghart! DeAnna edited my first book, and has been editing a column I write for http://www.ProjectConnections.com for many years. She's a comic genius, and even makes criticism fun! By some miracle she was able to shoehorn this project into the mountain of other responsibilities she juggles like a circus clown.

And then there are the folks at Happy About®. Wow! I can't afford the tip Liz Tadman deserves for managing this project, Mitchell Levy has been unreasonably supportive considering he is running an entire publishing company, and there are plenty of people behind the scenes who deserve a hearty pat on the back for all they did to bring this project to completion.

Finally, I'm grateful to my family and friends, who tolerated my inattentiveness during intense periods of editing, and my occasional grouchiness—which mostly is an old habit, but, far too frequently, I used working on this book as an excuse for my "dark side" slipping out. (Oops! Sorry about that! I sincerely hope that part of your butt grows back.)

Big, huge, gargantuan thanks, everyone!

- Kimberly

A Message From Happy About®

Thank you for your purchase of this Scrappy About book, a series from Happy About®. It is available online at: http://happyabout.com/scrappyabout/scrappywomeninbusiness.php or at other online and physical bookstores.

- Please contact us for quantity discounts at sales@happyabout.info.
- If you want to be informed by email of upcoming Happy About® books, please email bookupdate@happyabout.info.

Happy About is interested in you if you are an author who would like to submit a non-fiction book proposal or a corporation that would like to have a book written for you. Please contact us by email editorial@happyabout.info or phone (1-408-257-3000).

Other Happy About books available include:

- Scrappy Project Management®:
  http://happyabout.info/scrappyabout/project-management.php
- Scrappy General Management:
  http://bit.ly/scrappygm [3]
- Climbing the Ladder of Business Intelligence:
  http://www.happyabout.info/climbing-ladder.php
- Overcoming Inventoritis:
  http://www.happyabout.info/overcoming-inventoritis.php
- Collaboration 2.0:
  http://happyabout.info/collaboration2.0.php
- #LEADERSHIPtweet:
  http://www.happyabout.com/thinkaha/leadershiptweet01.php
- The Successful Introvert:
  http://happyabout.info/thesuccessfulintrovert.php
- Expert Product Management:
  http://www.happyabout.com/expertproductmanagement.php
- 42 Rules for Successful Collaboration:
  http://www.happyabout.com/42rules/successful-collaboration.php
- 42 Rules of Employee Engagement:
  http://www.happyabout.com/42rules/employee-engagement.php
- 42 Rules for Effective Connections:
  http://www.happyabout.com/42rules/effectiveconnections.php
- 42 Rules for Working Moms
  http://www.happyabout.com/42rules/workingmoms.php

---

3. www.happyabout.com/scrappyabout/scrappy-general-management.php

Contents

Kick Off—Sorry to Be So Serious, But...I Don't Find This Amusing Anymore

Scrappy Kimberly Wiefling
President, Wiefling Consulting, LLC
Global Business Leadership & Project
Management Consultant

"The absence of alternatives clears the mind marvellously."
- *Henry Kissinger*

Boy, Was I Lucky to Be Born a Girl!

I've been extremely fortunate to live during a time when opportunities for women expanded tremendously, and I've enjoyed the support of many Scrappy gal pals throughout my career and my life. I honestly believe that I would have been a complete failure, or at best mediocre, in my professional life without their encouragement, and without the many mentors—both men and women—who've generously shared their wisdom with me. And if I've traveled farther than my sisters of previous generations, it's because they hacked out a path that made my journey easier, experiencing challenges I've never had to face, and bearing burdens that I can't even imagine.

My favorite such story is from my dear friend Jane Evans, now in her eighties. She was the first woman to earn an electronics engineering degree from San Jose State University, and the first female engineering graduate hired by Hewlett Packard. She told me that as she approached graduation she received rejection letters from companies she didn't even apply to! If I remember correctly she added some cute little profanity like "those sunny beaches." Thank you, Jane! I can catch sight of my own future possibilities, and those of future generations of businesswomen, because I'm standing on your strong shoulders.

For a good chunk of my professional life I felt as if I struggled to achieve what others came by easily. At least that's how it seemed to me. I was especially impressed with the successful women I encountered in my technical field, perhaps because there were so few of them. My career path was haphazard; theirs appeared to be well planned and tidy. I groped my way along a torturous route to success; they seemed to glide up a career development staircase with the grace of a ballerina. My hair flew every which way like a rock star who'd been on the road one too many months; theirs was neatly coiffed. Sigh.

A Game You Just Can't Win

It turns out that was a bunch of nonsense! Life is messy, and careers are no exception. Appearances don't tell the whole story. But we tend to compare our insides to everyone else's outsides, which guarantees that we usually come up short. Aware of our own frailties, we judge ourselves harshly against the many examples of success around us. But it's a trick of the light, you see. I've found that most of the successful women I admire have an intriguing story to tell, and it's far from neat, clean, and tidy. It's a tale of challenges, hard work, struggles, best guesses, dead ends, wrong turns, course corrections, setbacks, persistence, and a touch of good luck, which finally brought them the success they so richly deserve.

When I grasped this, I felt a huge weight lift off of my shoulders. Suddenly I realized that I'd been in the grip of the Impostor Syndrome—a problem for many successful men and an epidemic among professional women. Interestingly, according to Impostor Syndrome studies, the more successful you are, the more likely that you'll suffer from this intriguing phenomenon! I now understand that, although some people make it look easy, in reality, the path to success is often as crooked as a lightening bolt. It's tempting to believe that the professionals surrounding us somehow have their act completely together while we lurch fitfully onward, but the real story is often much more complicated and chaotic.

The Impostor Syndrome was first reported in a research study by psychology professor Pauline Clance and psychologist Suzanne Imes in a paper entitled "The Impostor Phenomenon Among High Achieving Women" (1978). There's a helpful website on the topic (Of course, there is! Jumpin' Hay-zeus on a pogo stick, there's a website on pretty much everything by now.) by Dr. Valerie Young that promises to enable you to "feel as bright and capable as everyone seems to think you are" for as little as $19.[4] I've been amazed at how many people have never heard of the Impostor Syndrome, and, in spite of my irreverent tone, I've referred hundreds of people to this website. I haven't forked over the $19 yet, however, as my goal is to feel even brighter and *more* capable than everyone seems to think I am. So far I haven't found a website offering that. (It's probably blocked by my adult content filter.)

Many successful professionals—and women in particular—live in fear that one day they will be unmasked as the charlatans that they are. They dread that they may someday wake up to find that all of their

---

4. http://impostorsyndrome.com/

achievements have been nothing more than a collection of fortuitous coincidences. Revealed as a fraud, they'll slink into irrelevance. How positively dismal!

Hey, Ophelia, Wake Up!

I also read in *Reviving Ophelia* with a certain amount of shock about the deterioration of self-esteem in young girls as they "struggle to stay within a narrow definition of female."[5] My own personal experience is that the tear in the fabric of self-esteem during a woman's youth can widen into a gulf as we venture into the professional realm. (Maybe it happens for men, too. Sorry, I have no personal experience in that area! If you'd like to write *Scrappy Men in Business*, give me a shout. I'm open to the possibility.) In my case, the emotional burden of busting barriers was almost more than I could bear. On the outside I appeared strong, but inside I was lost, searching, and in need of camaraderie and support.

Working on this project has helped me to realize how lonely I've sometimes felt in the business world. In spite of my bravado, I've often felt overwhelmed and extremely inadequate. Watching other successful people who looked like they had it all together, I sometimes believed that I wasn't in their league because my path was somewhat unconventional or a bit erratic. It seemed to me that I lurched while others strode toward success. I'm grateful to the people in my life who believed in me enough to invest some of their time to build my confidence and help me find my way. I'm thankful for those who have shared their stories with me, including the authors in this book. I've found that sharing our life stories dispels the illusion of separateness between us. There are plenty of obstacles to business success without the little voice in our heads fighting us night and day!

---

5. Mary Pipher, *Reviving Ophelia: Saving the Selves of Adolescent Girls* (Ballantine Books, 1995), http://amzn.to/clbuUC (www.amazon.com/Reviving-Ophelia-Saving-Selves-Adoles-cent/dp/1594481881/ref=sr_1_1?ie=UTF8&s=books&qid=1276312178&sr=8-1)

I Don't Find This Stuff Amusing Anymore

It's just a hunch, mind you, but I don't believe that the collective talents of women are being fully utilized for the greater good of our businesses, our community, and our planet. I spent my adolescence feeling too strong to be feminine and too weak to make it in a man's world. Fortunately, one day I glimpsed what was possible, and the power that lay dormant within, through role models like the women in this book. But mining my potential came at a price, as do most things precious.

Disappointingly, after decades of increasing education levels and hard work, the progress of women in the professional world is nowhere near where I would have predicted it would be this far along into the 21st century. After twenty years of being painfully aware of women's position in the professional pecking order, I can sincerely say that I don't find this stuff amusing anymore.

Check out these stats from the January 2010 Catalyst "U.S. Women in Business" report:[6]

- Women in the U.S. labor force: 46.7%
- Women in management, professional, and related occupations: 51.4%
- Female Fortune 500 corporate officers: 13.5%
- Female Fortune 500 board seats: 15.2%
- Female Fortune 500 top earners: 6.3%

And here are some statistics from the May 2010 Catalyst "Women CEOs of the Fortune 1000" report:[7]

- Number of female CEOs of Fortune 500 companies: 15
- Number of female CEOs in Fortune 501-1000 companies: 14

Not a pretty sight—and not good news for the planet, either. Japan and Germany in particular will face at least a 20 percent shortage in

---

6. http://www.catalyst.org/publication/132/US-women-in-business
7. http://www.catalyst.org/publication/322/women-ceos-of-the-fortune-1000

working-age population in the coming decades.[8] It seems to me that we'll need everyone's help if businesses are going to successfully meet the challenges facing humanity.

Read One Chapter with a Glass of Chardonnay and Call Me in the Morning

Each chapter of this book is one women's fascinating perspective on what it means to be a Scrappy Woman in Business, and all of them are teeming with personal insights and practical tips to encourage you on your journey toward your own goals and dreams. Each of these women has travelled a very different road, but they all ended up in the "Scrappy Women in Business Hall of Fame" because they are ordinary people who created extraordinary results through sheer determination, willpower, and scrappiness. They could have easily thrown in the towel at any point and led easier (albeit far more boring!) lives. But they didn't. They kept going! By doing so, they demonstrated in eleven beautiful ways what's possible when you refuse to be "realistic."

Three Magic Wishes

1. It is my sincere hope that this book will ignite a flame inside of you that leaves you restless to discover what you're capable of.

2. I further hope that, after reading, you think to yourself, "Hey, if they can do it, so can I!"

3. Finally, and most importantly, I hope that you will take action with the intention of making a positive difference not only in your life, but for this planet.

---

8. Adele Hayutin, "Population Age Shifts Will Reshape Global Workforce," Stanford Center on Longevity, February 2010, http://bit.ly/cdqs6J (longevity.stanford.edu/files/SCL%20Workforce%20Shifts%20Handout%2002-10_FINAL_WEB.pdf.)

Even one tiny action each day is enough to make a difference. (Even a woman with a limp moves forward!) Remember, everything seems impossible until someone else does it. Then it's merely difficult.

Let's get busy!

- Scrappy Kimberly

Part I

We're Not Just *In* Business, We *Mean* Business

When I first joined the working wounded, my motivation was mainly to avoid living with my parents. My first real job was in the military, repairing electronics for the U.S. Air Force. This was a big step up from my high school career—mowing lawns and cleaning houses. I hadn't cut quite enough grass to save the dough needed for college, so I enlisted in the military right after graduation to get the educational benefits in the GI Bill. Not that I mulled the decision over for long, but I estimated that I was unlikely to be killed while in the military for the next few years because it was a relatively uneventful period in U.S. history. I was still doing a bit of fence sitting when the recruiter promised that I could "be all I could be," and they'd throw in a free wardrobe. Done deal!

If you knew me you'd say, "The military? You've got to be kidding!" For one thing, I hate taking orders. If I had been going ashore on D-Day I would have been asking, "Are you sure this is the best place to land this boat?" Needless to say, it was a terrible shock to my system, and it wasn't all that easy on the poor military either. But somehow we managed to get through it. I got a marksman's ribbon for being a good shot, and they tested me for drugs every couple of months to see if I was "using" or just hyperactive. (It was the latter.) Just defending the country wasn't a big enough task to keep me from getting bored, so while in the service I took on a whole string of odd jobs that reads like the rap sheet of some deadbeat drifter. I drove a tractor, worked as a gas station attendant, and gave fat people diet shots in their gluteus maximae, making time in my schedule for these extra jobs by polishing my combat boots using furniture spray instead of the time-consuming traditional process. It was all pretty dull (except for my boots) and just a way for a young, purposeless gal from the suburbs of Pittsburgh to earn some cash for college. Sure, there was the day I was almost hit by an F-4 fighter jet that crashed on the road that I was travelling to get to work, but I just swerved around it so I wouldn't be late. (I'm very punctual!)

After surviving the jet crash, military food, base housing, and postings in Texas, North Carolina, and Germany, I escaped with my honorable discharge clutched in my fist and headed to college. While in school, I began working part-time at a giant chemical company with lots of cool gadgets in their labs. I soon found that I was really jazzed about my work. My job was no longer just a way to make money. I became obsessed with excellence and threw myself into whatever task I was given, even relatively meaningless ones, as though the future of the world depended upon the quality of my performance. Imagine my surprise when this practice didn't earn me the love and affection of all of my colleagues! Cripes, some of them even took me aside and cautioned me, "Hey, slow down! You're making us look bad." (Yeah, right! Slowing down is for when you're dead!) Fortunately I worked with a couple of obsessively excellent peeps who encouraged me. (My boss actually had a habit of frequently shouting "Excellent!" at random moments.) Since it was just a temporary, part-time job, I didn't sweat the negative vibes from my underachieving colleagues. But I did learn the difference between a wage slave and someone who is passionately committed to excellence—a distinction that would become increasingly important to me.

These days I fancy myself the kind of person who can spot extraordinary professional commitment a kilometer away. I invited the women in this section to contribute their stories because I've been particularly impressed with their commitment to making a Godzilla-sized positive difference through their work. Hannah, Yuko, Pat, and Mai-Huong are on my list of "most admired businesswomen" because, no matter what their jobs, they operate as if they are on a mission that matters. They bring the intensity of an Olympic gold medalist to every task. They aren't just IN business, they MEAN business!

Catch a glimpse of their Scrappiness in these four chapters. As you read you will realize that their career paths were anything but a neat, clean promenade up the stairway of success. I find that's often the case with people I admire greatly—they have a rich and varied history, and the purpose of each stage of their life and career development isn't necessarily clear to them (or anyone else—parents, for example) as it occurs. But, through these diverse experiences and their intense commitment to excellence, they develop an unstoppable power to create extraordinary results out of the most unlikely raw materials.

There's an old saying: "When life gives you lemons, make lemonade." When life gives *these* women lemons, they're liable to set up an entire lemonade manufacturing and distribution system, with worldwide franchises and licensing agreements, and a global network for contacting extraterrestrials interested in partnering with them.

Sink into a hot bath and enjoy!

- Scrappy Kimberly

"Creative minds have always been known to survive any kind of bad training."
- *Anna Freud*

Hannah Kain

**President & CEO of ALOM Technologies
Corp., Mentor, Coach, Friend, Supporter,
Daughter, Wife, Sister, Aunt, Author, Chief
Jack-of-All-Trades and Chick-in-Charge**

*Scrappy Kimberly says: Many years ago, I hit
Hannah up for some guidance on business
leadership, and she offered, "Try not to kill
anyone." I've found her advice very practical over
the years, seeing how, from time to time, I've
wanted to strangle quite a few of my colleagues.
(And it's been more convenient to run my
business outside of prison, since it requires
travel.) But even more valuable has been
learning about the power of a Scrappy sense of
humor. Her sense of humor has been a life
preserver of resilience and sanity in a sea of
business lunacy.*

I was actually gainfully employed until 1997. Some of my jobs were like a Dilbert cartoon, and I figured: "Why not change my role in the cartoon?" Refusing to change my hairdo, I became the non-pointy-haired boss when I founded ALOM in 1997. My team and I have grown this company to become a leading global supply chain company headquartered in Fremont, California. Prior to founding ALOM in 1997, I held various management and executive positions, with a wide range of experience in the packaging industry dating back to 1990. I earned three university degrees (B.S. in political science, M.S. in communications, and M.B.A. in marketing), and I'm a frequent lecturer and speaker, and a published author of a popular textbook on market analysis, now in its fourth edition. It is by now outdated, and it is in Danish, so don't rush to buy it, but it was fun to write a textbook that was mandatory. And, no, I did not include any convoluted formulas to make future generations suffer like I did.

My unwavering focus is on customer delight and quality. This focus led to a successful ISO certification for ALOM within a year of starting the business and has fostered long-term business relationships. I have extensive international management experience including many plane trips and bad airline meals, and am involved in numerous governmental and educational agencies and business groups (read: constantly in meetings). I'm a board member of the National Association of Manufacturers (NAM) and Women's Initiative Silicon Valley, a nonprofit organization. I believe in giving back to the community. I have been so blessed by supportive men and women surrounding me and encouraging me with awards, such as 2009 Enterprising Woman of the Year. Thank you, all!

"Dream it, do it."
- *The Manufacturing Institute*

1 My Friend's Car, the Ladies' Room, and Other Career-Boosting Places

Hannah Kain

Scrappy Thoughts: *Almost every single job candidate I interview for a position in my company wants to run his or her own company. Some have already done so in the past, and others currently do so on the side while holding down another job. The entrepreneurial spirit is alive and kicking! Having your own company is a great experience. It is not right or wrong to want to start a company, jUSt like it is not right or wrong to be employed, or to have wild dreams. It is jUSt different. This chapter contains some random thoughts that may help those of you about to embark on the journey of running your own business. It recounts and celebrates my amazing journey doing exactly that, with a few surprising twists and turns along the way. Enjoy!* - Hannah

"The FBI is on the line," said the receptionist one morning, as I stepped into the company. "They need to talk to you." Now, even though I am not a morning person, that greeting will get anybody's mind kicked into high gear. My heart rate doubled, and my mind raced faster than the Indy 500. Yes, it was the FBI, and they were simply conducting an investigation concerning some minor fraud that one of our customers had been subjected to.

It was an unusual start to a day for sure. But every day is truly unique, and every day is challenging in its own way. And if it isn't challenging, I'll find a way to make it challenging. I just love the endless variety and rapid change in my work. Wearing many hats and being the jack-of-all-trades suits me. Yet, as the company has grown, I have enjoyed hiring really competent people to take over various functions to free up my time to focus on what I—right or wrong—believe is more important stuff.

My Journey

Life is a journey, and running a company is a kind of journey as well. Everyone in business talks about exit strategies and whether to cash out and all that jazz. I'm more concerned about enjoying the ride. I'm always peering ahead, trying to determine the next destination, steering to stay on course, and keeping all of my fellow travelers together. Some days I feel in control, driving the bus with a strong navigation system and lots of support. Other days feel more like I'm sitting in a random car on a remotely controlled roller coaster and pretending to have some kind of control. (Who is screaming in the background?)

My business adventures started at the ripe old age of four, when my brother and I formed a joint venture. We went to a nearby forest and dug up wild primroses. We loaded them onto our small toy cart, and then we started our door-to-door services, targeting garden owners based on the looks of their gardens. Our revenues were low, as was our pricing strategy, which was to charge around 10¢ per primrose. On the other hand, our cost of goods sold (COGS as I would later learn to call it) was zero, so we had a 100 percent profit margin. As always, when something is too good to be true, there's a hitch. Our dad did not want his children "begging in the neighborhood," and, thus, I got my first experience with business being hampered by authorities and regulations. After that, I learned to ask permission before I started anything new—at least until I turned eighteen.

My dad ran a small business on the side from our home. He was a college professor during the day and an entrepreneur by night. At age eleven, I became engaged in the business, and within a couple of years I was running most of it, except for anything to do with verbal negotiations. My dad was slightly hesitant to send a fourteen-year-old girl out to negotiate with lenders and so forth. I remember our somewhat conservative CPA coming to our home, and his obvious discomfort as he discovered that he had been dealing with a fourteen-to-fifteen-year-old girl all along. I learned business during those early years, and my interest in it easily outweighed any loss I felt from the many other activities that I had to forgo as a result.

By chance, I fell into politics when I was seventeen. My native country, Denmark, was a target for the Communist Bloc at the time, and the youth population was especially targeted. By that time the student organizations were heavily infiltrated, and, in reality, they were run out of East Germany—which, for those of you too young to remember, was then a separate country from West Germany. My best friend had been invited to a meeting by a group of students that wanted to revolt against the communist dominance. She had just gotten her driver's license, and we were excited about going on a trip together that Saturday.

This innocent road trip began my political career. Within five months, I was elected chair of the first of several new student organizations, and over the next five years I was heavily involved in running these volunteer associations. I learned to manage and motivate hundreds of volunteers. I hired my first paid staff at the age of nineteen. And I learned to negotiate and to be in the media spotlight. I did manage to get surprisingly good grades in spite of only studying whenever I could squeeze it in between my political responsibilities. But there is no doubt that I learned more from my extracurricular activities than from classrooms and textbooks. This was also where I met my husband. Fortunately, he had already seen me take charge, run things, and be away on trips at the most inopportune moments. What He Saw Was What He Got. That road trip in your friend's car really can lead to places.

Money

It comes in pretty handy sometimes, and you especially notice that fact if you didn't have any before. I put myself through university with a combination of temp work and income from political activities. For example, I wrote paid op-ed articles and gave speeches that sometimes were paid. Some of my current friends might justifiably be surprised to learn that I was hired for a long-term assignment on a weekly radio show about manners, where I represented the voice of manners among young people.

However, it was through clerical temp work that I made the most money. This allowed me to see business from the bottom up, and I do mean the very bottom. I observed close-up the pecking order of some companies, where new temps were kept at arm's length on the outside. Other companies were warm and welcoming. Some had well-trained staff. Some had lots of politics. I remember distinctly that I felt different about contributing in each of these different environments. While you can certainly learn about culture in business school, as I did, feeling it yourself makes an unforgettable impact. It's a lesson that has guided my business to this very day.

Some temp jobs were tedious, and I learned to grit my teeth and just do the work. I learned to keep myself listed with several temp agencies so I was assured a choice of income opportunities. At one point in my studies, I was so low on cash that I lived on $1.50 for two weeks. After enduring that experience, during which I tired of eating whatever was in the cans from my meager pantry and visiting friends and family at meal times, I decided that would never happen again. These days I sometimes think I'd benefit from a couple of weeks of such a diet, but I haven't been able to bring myself to relive those scary times—and, in any event, I tend to live a little healthier these days than in my happy-go-lucky youth.

It just so happened that I became very interested in computer programming, and had taken a few classes early on in the computer era. It was fun! Then word processing came out, and most secretaries froze in panic. Some even retired to escape the learning curve. Their IBM Selectric typewriters were about as advanced as they could handle. Because I was familiar with programming and did not panic at the sight of the computer, I was mostly viewed as a whiz and a saving angel when I arrived as the new company temp.

True to my practice of doing things differently, I graduated from my university in Aarhus, Denmark, while I was at the United Nations in New York as part of the Danish parliamentary delegation. I ran for parliament for the first time at the age of twenty-one. Regrettably, I was not elected, but my party offered me the chance to be at the UN for seven weeks to represent the party's parliamentary group. I finished my master's thesis before leaving for New York, and I received my grade and their hearty congratulations on my way to an official dinner at the Icelandic ambassador's residence.

The other lasting memory from that evening was that the ambassador started his speech just as the ice cream was being served. This being a formal diplomatic dinner, one is not supposed to eat during speeches, so we all watched the ice cream turn to slush and then to cold soup as he droned on. I don't recall a word from his speech. Timing is everything, especially with food lovers around the table. To make things worse, they had seated me next to my archenemy. I had made front-page news in my feud against a television anchor, as I had threatened to file an official complaint regarding his journalistic bias. Knowledge is everything when making seating arrangements. What an evening—archenemy at my side and melted ice cream. At least I miraculously had gotten my degree.

My time in politics and at the UN allowed me to meet many formidable leaders at an early age. Rubbing elbows with these people, I learned not to be star-struck. Instead, I was intent on learning how these great leaders focused on getting water to the world's population or on preventing child slavery while at the same time battling bureaucracy, politics, and even resistance from the very people they were trying to help. When looking back at my career, it might seem that my time in politics was a detour. In reality, it was a wonderful opportunity for a young person to meet extremely talented leaders. And it impacted me for a lifetime.

Never been in politics? I cannot recommend strongly enough for young people to obtain similar experiences. Volunteer, or be an intern, or get elected, as I did, and learn a lesson that will stay with you for life.

For many years after graduation, I was actually gainfully employed, by which I mean I worked in salaried jobs. I attempted to stay within entrepreneurial pockets in the companies I worked for and even had one job where my role was to help start and support new businesses. That job was exciting! On the other hand, I once worked for a more conservative company...for three weeks, until I quit. (Yuk!) Those who know me won't be surprised to find that it just was not a good fit. When I occasionally have an employee quit at an inopportune moment, I always think that it is the ghost of my former employer taking revenge on me for leaving their job after just three weeks.

"It's About Business, Not Emotions." Yeah, Right!

OK, it's time I confess. Back when I was an employee, I lied...for years ...about my job...to an important person—myself! I told myself that I treated my job as I would if I owned the company. I honestly thought that was true. I put in a lot of hours, and I diligently tried to do right by my employer. But nothing could have prepared me for the emotional change I experienced from running my own company—the anxiety, the involvement, sometimes even anger, but also the pride, the thrill, and the vision. There's nothing like owning your own company to make you treat the job as if you own the company.

I know, I know: "It is about business, not about emotions." Don't you believe it for a second! Business is emotional. Starting, running, and growing a business is about being passionate and caring, yet not giving a damn. Yes, you need money, buildings, servers, and people. You need vendors and customers. But more than anything else, you need passion.

Without passion, you lose. Your passion is the spirit that will drive your persistence, ignite your staff, and persuade your customers. The list of bad stuff happening in any given company on any given day is long: staff members may get sick at crucial moments, they may abuse the system, some don't follow directions, and some may turn on you and even steal from you. Authorities may make your life miserable with endless bureaucracy, rules, and lack of cooperation, or the all-too-rare commodity, common sense. Customers may be unreasonable and nitpicky, pay you late or even never, not appreciate the work, or needlessly harass your employees. Vendors may flunk, fail to deliver, or fold. You might spend your time on endless paperwork to get your certifications, comply with laws, feed the lawyers, satisfy the bank's thirst for information, and cover your behind. In short, the pile of adversity that any company owner or CEO faces is as high as the day is long. I know, because I have lived it. In the end, what makes me keep going is my passion around the vision. Sure, there are also plenty of hardworking, honest, smart, and supportive people that keep you going. And there are wonderful customers who truly appreciate what you are doing for them. And, of course, there are friends and an extensive support network that everyone should have around them. But in the end, your passion is the driver. You need to be passionate about your vision and the journey. If I had to name one thing that makes the difference for a company's success, it is the passion of the CEO. Like oxygen, you have to have it to survive.

Why, then, is it a requirement also to "not give a damn?" Because you need to let go of what people think. Unlike running for political office, you are not subject to the popular vote. When leading your own business you will have to make a lot of decisions that you have to shoulder alone. For example, when you terminate an employee (by that I mean fire, not the ultimate "termination"), you cannot explain the reasoning behind the termination to the world. People may think you unfair and cold, when in fact you were extremely justified. Sometimes you also just need to follow your gut.

Everybody else may be telling you one thing—but you deeply sense that something else is right for you. That's not been a problem for me. I've always enjoyed swimming against the stream. Back in 1985, I won an award that is given annually by one of Denmark's greatest businessmen. He and I had barely met—yet he had captured my personality well enough that, when he presented me the award, he spoke about having selected me because I swim against the stream "like the salmon." I never forgot the speech. Today, I enjoy helping young business people—most of whom are women—because I remember what a boost that speech gave me. Somehow, I felt it gave me permission to be different.

Most of US are obsessed with fitting in. We treat life as one big campaign for the approval of others. But we are really all very different. I remember being extremely anxious about not fitting in. In fact, the Danish culture is based on fitting in. Remember how the "ugly duckling" is ostracized in the fairy tale by Hans Christian Andersen? Perhaps that's why I enjoy being in the US, and especially in Silicon Valley. Here you "fit in" by being different.

About Risk and Living

My dad was declared dead eleven years before I was born. He officially died in a "Konzentration Camp" (KZ Camp). He would later tell the story about smuggling weapons into the camp, getting caught, and being sentenced to die. Waiting for his execution in a small, obscure hole in the ground, he was overlooked when troops liberated the camp and only found later. The troops thought that he had already been executed, and he was listed as the last person to die in the camp. In reality, he was the last rescued survivor. After his rescue, he learned that his family had been killed, except for some distant relatives.

I can't imagine what my dad felt about going from a near miss of his own death to the news of the death of his family. I haven't had to face anything near the risks he faced in those dark times. I have found that everybody looks at risk differently. For me, the story of death and close misses is also the story about living life to its fullest...to fulfill dreams...to celebrate...and to put risk in perspective. My dad's story helps me do so.

"What would you do if you knew you couldn't fail?" This is one of those standard business questions that coaches ask and that are good to think about. Yet it's difficult, because you know that you may actually fail. In my opinion, you cannot succeed if you are not willing to risk failing, because the only way to avoid risking failure is to avoid being in the game. Maybe the biggest failure of all is not to try. Maybe I will choose that as my epitaph. One thing's for sure, mine will never be along the lines of, "Should have, could have, wish I would have, if only ...." Better to give it everything I've got. Better to give it my very best.

Don't go shedding any tears for me, but sometimes it is lonely at the top, and anxiety can kick in. "Uneasy lies the head that wears a crown," wrote Shakespeare in *Henry IV*. I counter that unease with friends, associations, and my membership in Vistage International, which provides me with a business coach and a peer group of business owners I can rely on for advice and support. My Vistage friends are of tremendous importance to me.

I also take action to stay on track. I have 1-on-1 meetings with my coach, and I also, perhaps surprisingly, have 1-on-1 meetings with myself—looking at my goals, reviewing whether I am on track, and whether I am spending my time wisely. (Maybe I should call these 0.5-on-0.5 meetings, or 1-on-0 meetings!) And every morning, I ask myself what my most important goal is for that day. This simple practice helps me stay focused on what really matters to me.

Tolerance for stress and anxiety can be learned. The bar keeps moving up, and it simply takes a higher level of adversity or disruption to throw you off balance. Issues that turned my world upside down ten years ago hardly impact me at all anymore. But if you absolutely hate taking risk, running your own business may not be for you. You may also be in trouble running your own business if you are the kind of person who takes risk just for the heck of it. It is a roller coaster ride, but the car does not always stay on the tracks. So, while being risk-averse is real drawback for a business owner, taking extraneous risks may not be a great idea either.

A Woman and a CEO

There is an old joke about how tough it is to get older, yet it is better than the alternative. I am asked all the time how I feel about being a female CEO, and it cracks me up, because it is probably better than the alternative. Truthfully, I never tried to be dead, and I also never tried to be male. Not that it wouldn't be interesting to try the latter for a very, *very* short while—in fact, one of my more far-flung business ideas includes travel into other people's bodies. (And now you know why my husband almost never pays any attention when I make my frequent outburst: "I have a new business idea...." But, I digress—which, by the way, is a very female trait.)

I have been discriminated against for any number of reasons I am sure, from being fat to being foreign. Oh, and I do not have any of those coveted Y chromosomes. To the irritation of the men around me, I sometimes ask men to do things that require a Y chromosome, such as getting a quote from a car repair shop.

I've changed my perspective on being discriminated against. I used to get so angry. Now I get even instead—or better than even. It happens that men underestimate me. I really enjoy that. You can practically see my hair turn blonder and blonder during such a meeting. I have a pink scarf for these situations. So, at the second meeting, I will wear my pink scarf. It is the equivalent of war paint. It reminds me to keep my mind focused on what I can gain from the fact that this person is underestimating me. I ought to deduct the expense for that pink scarf—it made me a lot of money.

Interestingly enough, women are extremely powerful in the business world. Depending on which study reports the influence, women control between 60 and 85 percent of all purchase decisions both at home and in the business world, leaving men to control between 40 and 15 percent (at that level, why even bother). What an opportunity for a female business owner! In front of me are female decision makers, many of whom are dreaming of starting their own company. They really want to support me. They identify with who I am and what I am doing. I have clinched deals in the ladies' room (though usually we do not sign contracts by passing them under the stalls), and I embrace the strong support network among women. In Silicon Valley that network is so strong and supportive that men often want to become part of it.

Many men, of course, have no idea what they miss out on, like the guy who kept asking me what my husband might be thinking regarding a business decision I was making. The truth is that my husband lived in blissful ignorance and total indifference that such a decision was even in process. But the third time this guy asked, I decided that I could not establish a working relationship with him. I was forced to go with his competitor. He lost a contract that by now is worth way over $10 million. Game over.

Let's end this section with a huge hurrah to the men who get it! We women love doing business with you, and I have scarves in many colors, so don't be alarmed if I wear one.

My Gut—A Great Asset

I am pig-headed; ask anyone who knows me. I am also a terrible listener; ask my husband. Oh, I *hear* what others are saying, to be sure. I even solicit input all the time—but in the end, I do my own thing and follow my own gut instinct. I've learned that there is nothing wrong with gut instinct. In fact, I have paid dearly to hone my gut instinct and continue to invest in it. It costs money and focus, takes time for reflection, and requires enormous self-confidence. When everyone else tells me that something is fine, but I feel that nagging doubt—do I have the courage to explore the doubt in spite of all the legwork and analysis done by the others? You bet! Why? Because almost every single time I went with the majority instead of my gut, my gut was right.

Forget business advice. It's almost always wrong, irrelevant and misguiding. If you follow the advice of the thirty thousand authors getting their business books published each year, are you better off? Nobody knows. What we do know is that many authors write about companies, examples, and situations that ended disastrously. I am reminded of a particular book that one unfortunate friend recommended a couple of years back. I read it on the plane on my way over to visit him, and he never heard the end of it, as one of the chapters was dedicated to the greatness of Enron. The Enron scandal had unraveled just two months prior to my reading the book. Another notorious company, SAS (Scandinavian Airlines), generated several management gurus touting great customer service. Now they charge for water. Anecdotal evidence abounds: there is no guarantee that the advice dished out in these books, or even *this* book, works.

Ultimately, advice has to be filtered in the light of each situation. I am not running GE, so Jack Welch's advice does not necessarily apply to my company. Advice is situational. But even more important, advice is personal. If I'm going to follow some management guru's advice, it needs to ring true with my values and goals. I still read business books, but I'm ruthless in sorting sort out what advice I take.

So, feel free to give me advice and tell me what you think. In fact, I encourage you to do so! But don't get offended if I don't take your advice. That's just who I am.

Compassion and Trust

There was a young man on a tram in Copenhagen. He looked terrible. His clothes were in shambles, and he spoke in broken Danish. When the conductor realized that the young man was penniless (or, more accurately in Danish currency, øre-less) and did not even have a ticket, he decided to throw him off the tram.

That young man was my dad returning from KZ camp. Because he had been found so late during the liberation of the camp, the famous White Buses used to transport KZ prisoners back to their families had already departed. My dad, who was now without a family, was left without any reasonable way to leave the horrible place where he had spent a significant part of his youth. He had to hitchhike plane rides through postwar Europe to make it back to Denmark, where friendly farmers had hidden him from the Nazis during the first part of the war.

As the conductor was getting ready to toss my dad off the tram, a stranger intervened. He not only paid my dad's tram ticket, but he also made sure he got to his final destination. My dad never forgot the kindness and generosity of the stranger. I learned about compassion from my dad's story.

My childhood home was filled with strangers seeking help from my dad. He was always happy to help them. Many strangers became successful with Dad's help, and eventually became friends. My mother was the same way, always trying to support and help her students. She was a teacher in a socially disadvantaged neighborhood at a time when few resources were available to support abused students and those from broken homes. I learned about helping others from my parents' superb example.

Me, I love to see people around me succeed. I happily give people chances to grow. I will invest time and money in seeing my staff and others make a better life for themselves. I recently joined the Women's Initiative (http://www.womensinitiative.org) to help disadvantaged women start their own companies. Some of my staff members say that I am being taken advantage of when I give people that extra chance. They are right! There are certainly always people taking advantage of any generosity. There are always people abusing trust. But, then again, there are other people who succeed just because of that one supportive conversation or that one person believing in them.

I hope I never stop believing in people. Being taken advantage of is a small price to pay for being true to my values as a human being. Compassion and trust are two very important factors in who I am.

My Best Decision

I am lucky. Some of the luck just happened, and some of the luck required a fight. I guess it is lucky that I love a fight! I'm in an industry that is changing by the minute. I have to reinvent myself and the company all the time. When I started the company in 1997, 55 percent of our revenue came from duplicating 3.5-inch floppy diskettes. (Does anyone even remember those? I know some of you were born after they became obsolete.) Since then, the company has changed dramatically, and many times. We now provide supply chain services globally in fourteen locations for large customers. It has been a wonderful journey. It requires that I stay alert. (No falling asleep at the wheel for this CEO!)

Recently, I was on a panel at a women's conference. The panel was asked what their best business decision was. The answer was easy for me. It is the decision that I will make tomorrow. If I stop believing that, it is time to hang it up. But there was one past decision that could qualify as a close second place. Why not just have fun and enjoy life? Roller coaster, here we come, martini in hand!

Yuko Shibata

**Strong and Gentle, Small-But-Mighty
Executive Director of ALC Education, Inc. of
ALC Group, Tokyo, Japan**

*Scrappy Kimberly says: Many people might be
fooled into thinking that this Scrappy woman is a
timid, quiet Japanese lady. But let me assure you
that Yuko Shibata is a tidal wave of change
sweeping over the island of Japan, with
far-reaching ripples extending throughout the
world. Meeting her changed the course of my
career forever, and I would never be foolish
enough to think that there's anything at all this
incredible business leader couldn't achieve.*

My name is Yuko and I was born in Japan, where many people call me "Shibata-san." I grew up in a small town called Kishima about an hour's train ride outside of Tokyo, where I still live to this day. I earned my degree in psychology in the U.S. from the University of Washington, Seattle, before returning to Japan. After working in Tokyo for Libyan and American companies, I decided that I wanted to work in an education-related field, so I got a job as a counselor for study-abroad programs and programs offering English study in Japan.

Seeing the trends in the international business world, I became very interested in preparing Japanese businesses for globalization, a field I have been working in for the past twenty-four years. Presently, I'm the Executive Director of the Program Management Division of ALC Education, Inc. Over the past five years, we've introduced a wide range of truly innovative and transformative global business leadership and management programs to Japanese companies through our collaboration with Kimberly Wiefling and her colleagues.

"Even if I knew that tomorrow the world would end, I would still plant my apple tree today."
- *Martin Luther*

2 The Unstoppable Power of Persistence

Yuko Shibata

Although I've lived all my life in Japan, where society's expectations and treatment of women differ greatly from those of men, I've lived anything but a traditional Japanese woman's life. As a young girl growing up in a small town, a long train ride from the center of Tokyo, I embraced two opposing dreams. On the one hand, I imagined that I'd grow up, get married, and have five children. At the same time, I dreamed of becoming a doctor, lawyer, or some person of significance in the business world. Looking back, straddling both of those possible futures ended up diluting my resolve to follow either one, and it wasn't until much later in my life that I found my true calling—to contribute to the global changes that are happening in the exciting world that we share.

Rich Is Fun, but Poor Makes You Strong

I was born on October 24, 1956—only eleven years after Word War II ended—the youngest of four children. Most people in Japan were poor at that time, and there were still many scars from the war. Although I do not remember much, I can see hints of those scars in the pictures taken of me as a child.

My father was a liberal thinker compared to most other Japanese men at that time. He was an active member of the Communist Party, helping to improve the treatment of workers who were not treated fairly. Because of this work, he was arrested, jailed, and subsequently lost his job. But my father was not a quitter. He started his own construction company after gaining some experience in the industry. Since this was an era of strong economic growth in Japan, my father's company grew successfully along with this wave, and my family eventually became one of the richest in our town. As I made my way through school, I enjoyed a very comfortable life compared to my classmates, who remember that I was the first to own an electric pencil sharpener and a western-style bed in my very own room. My family was also one of the first to purchase a color TV and a car with an automatic transmission—truly the height of luxury at the time!

My life suddenly changed again when I was in junior high school. My father lost about 300 million yen (around 3 million U.S. dollars) in a speculative venture, and his company almost went bankrupt. Our house was about to be seized, but his brother and friends helped him, so we avoided that catastrophe. My father continued to run the company on a very small scale, but never recovered financially from this enormous setback. This was a huge change and had a big impact on my life—ultimately positive. Many years later I said to my father, "If you had not lost the money, I wouldn't have gone to college in the U.S.A., and wouldn't have been able to become the successful business person that I am now. I would have ended up being a spoiled and lazy woman. Thank you!" I remember that he was a little surprised by my gratitude. But I think he understood exactly what I meant. Life is very interesting, and we frequently don't know whether something that happens to us is good or bad until we see the result down the road.

Sure, I Was Smart, But...

During my elementary and junior high school years, I was always among the top three students in the class, and always in a leadership position such as class president or captain of the volleyball club. But, looking back, I'm not sure if I was popular among friends. I was a typical straight-A student from a rich family. My friends did not know what happened to my family—that wasn't something you want people to know about! I remember noticing that the hardships in my family's life helped me become a better person, or at least inspired me to aspire to be a better person.

In junior high, I started to worry about saving my family the cost of continuing my education. I knew my family would not be able to afford the expensive tuition of a private high school, so I applied to only one public high school. I remember feeling a little scared about whether I would be accepted, and that perhaps I would end up with no school at all. Fortunately, I was accepted, and this high school was ranked among the top five in our area. That meant I could get a great education without costing my family any money. This was a big relief for me as a kid!

Although I was certainly capable of it, I was not a good student in my high school years. Instead, I spent those years as a drama queen, using my family situation as an excuse for not studying. My original desire was to become a medical doctor, one who could help as many people as possible. Then I found out I was not doing well in chemistry and physics, so I gave up all hope on that dream, and any thought of going into any career related to science in any way. Unfortunately, my attitude slump continued through the end of high school. Being a teenager can be like that, I guess. Although I've since become a very successful business executive, at that time it didn't look like I was going to have much success in my life. Of course, sometimes teenagers can be wrong, even though they think they're always right!

After graduation, my thinking went something like this: "Too bad I can't go to university, because we don't have any money. I'll just have to work after graduating from high school in order to save money for college." And that's what I did. I worked fourteen hours a day in a jazz club for about two years in order to save enough money to go to college in Japan.

College in Japan is generally quite relaxed and enjoyable for non-science majors—not at all the tough challenge it can be in some countries. Most of my friends from high school were enjoying their college life, and I started wondering if it would be worth spending my hard-earned money just to have fun. I was extremely tired most of the time, and feeling very negative about everything. Working so many hours a day left me exhausted and in a perpetual state of self-pity. Even saving every yen for school still wasn't going to be enough to get me into a good Japanese university. It wasn't just the cost; I was too tired to study for the extremely challenging entrance exams required by good private universities.

One Ticket to Anywhere Cheap, Please!

I'd never thought about leaving Japan, but I was feeling very stuck and wanted to change my life dramatically. One night a friend at the jazz club where I worked mentioned the idea of studying English abroad for a couple of months. That got me thinking about going to an English language school in the U.S., and I soon found myself applying for a student visa. The language schools I checked into didn't care about entrance exams. In fact, there didn't seem to be any requirement at all except a copy of my bank statement to prove that I'd have enough money to pay them, and a promise that I would return to Japan after my studies. It was decided! I would start changing my life by changing where I lived. But it turned into quite a bit more than just a couple of months studying English abroad.

After giving up my dream of becoming a medical doctor, I had considered being a psychologist to help people with mental problems. As I contemplated studying in the U.S., I remembered this dream. At that time, the field of psychology was much more advanced in the West, so it made sense to study abroad. America seemed to be a way to get unstuck and change my life. With very little research, I selected Seattle as my new home because the living expenses there were relatively low at the time (1977). I arrived in the U.S. just after the end of the Vietnam War and in the midst of the women's movement.

When I first arrived, I attended an English language school for six months. My English proficiency was low because I didn't study English at all after graduating from high school. I am very embarrassed to say that my English test results were so bad that I had to start at the lowest possible level. But I applied myself diligently to my studies, and was able to skip a few levels, leaving at the end of the six months at almost the highest level.

Budget continued to be a major factor in my decisions, so I applied to a community college, where the quarterly fees allowed me to take as many classes as I could handle for a fixed price. Continuing without a break from quarter to quarter, I sometimes took as many as 27 credits at a time. Through a combination of good planning, lots of studying, and a clear goal of getting into a good university as quickly as possible, I managed to accumulate over 90 credits in just five quarters with an excellent GPA.

Less than two years after my arrival in the U.S., I applied to the University of Washington, Seattle—one of the best schools in the region. Equipped with my lofty GPA, an impressive TOEFL (Test of English as a Foreign Language) score, my SAT results, and a "slightly adjusted" high school transcript (which I obtained with the help of a sympathetic teacher from my youth), I was accepted as a junior in the Psychology Department. It wasn't any easier than working in the jazz club, but at least I felt like I was going somewhere.

Education Doesn't Just Happen in School

Living in the U.S.A. was a valuable experience, and enabled me to explore a totally different culture and meet people from all over the world. Getting to know veterans of the Vietnam War in the shared housing where I lived opened my mind to the realities of the broader world. Many curious people asked me about the culture of Japan, which sparked thoughts about aspects of my own culture that I'd never previously considered. Meeting people from many different countries inspired me to study the history of Japan in relationship to the world.

This was a time of great change for the women's liberation movement. Women were aggressively demanding their rights. I was aware of the necessity of this movement because of the situation in the business world in Japan. (Men dominated the business world, and women worked for lower salaries for the same jobs, were unlikely to be promoted, were expected to leave after a few years to get married and have children, and were assumed to be working merely to find a husband anyway—I could go on and on....) But I had mixed feelings about the way in which some of the more radical feminists were going about it. While I was of course supportive of the concept of women having the same rights as men, I didn't want to become a man to achieve it. My study of history had convinced me that the aggressiveness of men had been responsible for much of the strife in the world, and I felt strongly that women should not adopt the ineffective strategies of men in order to succeed in business.

In the midst of all of this excitement, I encountered obvious racial discrimination for the first time in my life. I inquired about an apartment for rent, but was told it was taken. Suspecting it might have been because I was Japanese, I designed an experiment and enlisted the help of several friends to carry it out. We sent one of my black friends, who inquired about renting the apartment and was also told it was no longer available. When we sent one of our white friends, the apartment owner welcomed him warmly. It was surprising to me that this kind of attitude still existed in the U.S. Meeting a few Korean people during my time in the U.S. made me realize that this kind of attitude was still alive and well in Japan, too, where racial tensions between Japan and Korea persist to this day. Reading about such things in a book was one thing, but here I was living it.

I started to think about the reality of the situation and let go of my somewhat idealistic assumptions about people. My studies in behavioral psychology helped me to put all this in perspective. In school I was learning that people can experience the same thing in very different ways. For the next few years I had a heightened awareness of the different perspectives of other people, and I took great care with how I communicated, preferring to listen to others rather than to freely share my own somewhat naïve ideas about life. These experiences had a huge impact on my life and influenced me to do the work I am doing now, which is to bring people together in the business world from many different cultures to work together to solve the problems of our world.

Ever focused on money, I worked while I went to college, first doing small jobs like babysitting, and later doing office work and research studies. In typical Japanese style, I was very hardworking and task-oriented, and the speed and precision of my work were qualities absent in many college-aged student workers. As a result, I was very popular in all of the jobs I held during that time, a tradition that I have upheld through my career, although most people would describe me as anything but a typical Japanese businessperson.

Tokyo Job Hopper

Working and studying at the same time left me feeling uninspired about going to graduate school, so I returned to Japan with my B.A. in psychology and no money. At that time, someone with a university degree from another country was not considered an attractive candidate for a Japanese company. In the 1980s, Japanese businesses sought employees who would fit into and conform to the existing culture, and someone with my breadth of worldly experience certainly didn't show promise in conforming to current norms.

Initially I took a job with a company funded by a wealthy Libyan businessman. Frequent visits from the owner convinced me that his goal was to have a mistress in every country in the world, so I left after one year. My job wasn't interesting at all, so I didn't mind moving on. Although I knew that I wasn't likely to enjoy the financial industry (to me, nothing could be more boring!), I found a good paying job with an American financial company, Solomon Brothers. After one month, I realized that I wanted to do something with human beings, so I started searching for a job in the education industry.

The economy was very difficult at that time, but I managed to find a position at an English language school in Tokyo where my work and life experiences were considered a plus. Although I was supposed to be a counselor, my real job was to sell the programs to the people I was "counseling." I didn't know it at the time, but I am a born salesperson, and my sales skills would become extremely valuable to me as my career progressed.

The work was demanding, but that would have been okay if only I had believed in the services we were offering. In fact, people were paying us just to have a conversation with one of our good-looking native English speakers, for whom we loosely used the term "instructor." But just chatting with a native speaker doesn't make you a better communicator in English. True to my pattern to date, I quit within two years.

This wasn't what I had expected after getting a college education! After all those years of hard work to obtain an education, I had hopped from one job to the next without much to show for it. (Little did I know that this kind of career experience was a terrific preparation for what would become my life's work.) It was time for another trip abroad to catalyze another big change in my life, so I escaped to the U.S. on a tourist visa. I made my way on tips from jobs in Japanese restaurants owned by Korean people who kindly overlooked the fact that that I wasn't supposed to work while being a tourist. For all of my education, I was making more money than ever by being a waitress! But that quickly wore thin, and I returned to Japan and resurrected my career in the education services industry, where I've been working ever since.

In the beginning, I was most interested in English language skills and cross-cultural awareness, but I grew to realize that a set of core human skills unites us across linguistic, cultural, and other boundaries. English and cultural awareness are tools, but true breakthroughs in communication, and in building relationships, occur when people can walk in another person's shoes and connect on a heart level.

Going Global

Over the next two decades of my career, I worked for one of the biggest companies in this industry at the time. I was responsible for establishing alliances with educational institutions outside of Japan and sending thousands of Japanese businesspeople (mostly men) overseas to experience firsthand what it meant to be an international business professional. I was quickly promoted to manager and received a dizzying series of raises—most of which were kept secret because they came much faster than was typical for a person in my position. Now I was finally making more than I did as a waitress!

Our company already had a location in Houston, which isn't high on the list of places people in Japan hope to visit. I was chosen to oversee our expansion on the East Coast in our Washington, D.C., office in Virginia, which enabled me to make many trips there over the next five years. From my base in D.C., I traveled all over the U.S., visiting potential partner schools that would offer our services. Sounds exciting, doesn't it? But most of what I saw consisted of the inside of airplanes, taxis, and hotels. However, I did get a feel for how tough it was to be a global businessperson. Picking up and moving from one city to the next in a foreign country, being far from family and friends, traveling from hotel to hotel, I gained an appreciation for the human challenges that our clients faced as their companies grew internationally.

I learned to be ready for anything, and to take the unexpected in stride. Often things don't go as planned. Suitcases went one way and my airplane went another. Flights were canceled, leaving me without a place to stay for the night. Rooms were sometimes filthy, and the bar sometimes closed before the stresses of the day had been dulled by a sufficient quantity of the dry martinis I enjoyed at the end of a long day. Through it all, I managed to enjoy the little miracles and pleasures that I encountered along the way. And I learned a lot and grew strong. In particular, I gained the ability to quickly make decisions and adjust to whatever situation I found myself in. Now, whenever it seems that things are going wrong, I look for the nuggets of wisdom or personal growth available in the situation. "Never give up!" has become a guiding philosophy of my life.

Over the years, trends toward the "internationalization" of Japanese businesses turned into the now-popular "globalization" movement. Through it all, I continued to support this growth through educational and experiential programs that broadened the minds of participants. Just going abroad doesn't necessarily result in acquiring a global mindset, however, so we developed programs that included real-world experiences, tough challenges, and rich opportunities for people to grow as human beings as well as business leaders. Seeing the changes in their faces convinced me that we were doing the right things to enable them to be ready for the changes and challenges ahead. I was finally doing something I could really believe in!

Some Days You Just Can't Imagine What's Waiting for You

After twenty-three years of working in the industry, I was finally promoted to an executive position. On that particular day, I was invited to a meeting with the founder and CEO of our company and was told about the promotion. This was an especially big deal because I was the first woman within our company to be promoted to an executive position, what we call being a "board member" here in Japan. The promotion wasn't based on age or seniority, as is still the case in some Japanese companies. The overseas programs we'd been running had grown into global programs in Japan, taught by consultants from abroad, and the revenues and profits of this new business had grown significantly over the past couple of years. Our success was undeniable, and I think my promotion was a direct result of that, and of my ability to communicate effectively in complicated circumstances where many parties need to reach an agreement to achieve some desired result. Some people say that I single-handedly started this new area of our business, which now accounts for the fastest-growing part of our business. But I'm mature enough to know that no one does something of this magnitude alone, and I owe much of the success to the wonderful people who have been on this journey with me. (Nevertheless, I always enjoy hearing how people appreciate my contribution to this work!)

Later that same day, I received my diagnosis of breast cancer. Wow, two shocks in one day—one so incredibly wonderful, and the other a serious blow to my well-being. Because I believe in keeping hope alive, I started to wonder what this would make possible for my people, our business, and me. This kind of illness can give you time to really think about your life, and I thought about it that way. After years of tending to do everything myself, I started delegating more to others. And I looked for ways in which my experience with cancer could be an opportunity for my team to grow into greater leadership roles. I spent many hours thinking about the meaning of my life and what I wanted to accomplish in the time that I have left on this earth. I am lucky in that my work enables me to follow my destiny while earning a living—a luxury few people enjoy. This experience changed me, and through this I've learned that people can change. Now I feel more strongly than ever that things that seem impossible often aren't. I strive daily to communicate this to my people and to our clients so that they can achieve all that's possible for them, too.

I'm still holding on to my dream of helping to usher in the changes that Japanese businesses need to make in order to help solve the problems of our world. I even have the audacity to imagine that I might somehow be contributing in some way to world peace through my work. Of course, the world has so many problems that I also sometimes wonder whether one small Japanese businesswoman can make any difference at all. Although I've been tempted to give up many times, my belief has grown stronger since I've started building my Scrappy mental muscles. Now I'm guided by the inspiration that I first heard from my friend, Scrappy Kimberly Wiefling: "What seems impossible is often merely difficult." And I understand the importance of inspiring others. Personally, I'm doing whatever I can to help in my own way to contribute to a greater purpose than my own life here on earth. I hope you'll join me in that adventure. It's exciting!

Pat Obuchowski

**CEO (Chief Empowerment Officer!),
inVisionaria**

Scrappy Kimberly says: Pat Obuchowski is bound and determined to squeeze every juicy drop out of life! This Scrappy woman refuses to be shaped by her environment. Rather, she is a shaper of this world and is most definitely playing a much bigger game in life than most people can imagine for their short existence on this earth. I can't remember when I've met someone who celebrated the opportunity to live life fully the way Pat does. She's spreading exhilaration through the world. Watch out for her wake when she sails by!

I believe that when you own your own company you can give yourself any title you want. I am the CEO (Chief Empowerment Officer) of inVisionaria and a Scrappy Businesswoman whose passion is to coach other Scrappy women (or Scrappy wannabes) to be Scrappy leaders in our world. We need them.

I have a long bio because I've lived a full life, but it's not written on this page. You can read it all in my story. My life escape is DUI—Dancing Under the Influence (of loud music)—while driving my convertible with the top down and my trusted dog, Maggie, at my side.

"Work like you don't need the money, love as if you've never been hurt, dance as if no one is watching."
- *Satchel Paige*

"Sing as if no one is listening, laugh as if you were a child, believe as if the world depended on it."
- *Pat Obuchowski*

3 "What Do You Want to Be When You Grow Up?"

Pat Obuchowski

As a young girl, I would always cringe when this question was asked of me. The problem was I never really knew if I wanted to grow up or not! Of course, I had no choice in the matter of growing up. It was going to happen. But I did have a choice in what I wanted to be. Throughout my career, I've set my sights on one career dream after another—sometimes materializing them seemingly out of sheer intention, and usually with a bit of synchronistic luck. If you think you've wandered in your career path, take heart! You are not alone.

I Think I'll Be a Nun

As a young girl, I was confident I was going to be a nun. I went to a Catholic grammar school and high school, so the women I was always looking up to (both literally and figuratively) were nuns. But I soon realized I was not cut out for the nunnery when I discovered that I enjoyed drinking (I had some beers at the back of the bus on the way to Girl Scout camp. Got kicked out for that.) And that I really liked boys. Good decision on my part, and fortunate for the Catholic Church, too, I'm sure.

OK, Maybe I'll Be a Sports Coach

When I joined the volleyball team in grammar school, my role model became Mrs. Schilling, our coach. Mrs. Schilling was unique, as she was a former roller derby queen. Seriously. She was a Scrappy woman who taught us all about the importance of working with a team, both as a team member and a team leader. Most importantly, she taught us to be proud of our bodies and to use them athletically. So, of course, I decided that I wanted to be a sports coach. After all, they could drink and they were allowed to like boys. But when Mrs. Schilling told me how hard it was, and how little she was paid, it lost much of its appeal.

I'm Quite Sure I Was Born to Be a Teacher

When I got to high school, I *knew* my true calling was to be a teacher. I figured it was like being a nun, only you got to wear your own choice of clothing. I joined the Future Teachers of America and became the president of the club. We put on an "International Day" to raise money for the club, selling foods typical of other countries. I was in charge of the U.S.A. booth. After organizing the event and making twenty-five pounds of Sloppy Joes (that's what real American food was back then), I realized I didn't want to do anything like this again. So I quit the organization, decided to be a journalist instead, and joined the high school newspaper. I never got close to a Sloppy Joe after that.

No, Wait, I'll Be a Journalist!

Soon after, I went off to college, feeling very optimistic that journalism—more like photojournalism—was my calling. As it played out in my head, I imagined that I'd report the human experience in war-torn countries. I could almost hear the shells going off in the distance and smell the smoke as I reported from amidst the rubble of some neighborhood demolished by a recent battle. Determined to follow my dream, I applied to a world-class journalism school. I was accepted, but then reality set in. It didn't take me long to realize that I had no access to even come close to the money needed to pay for this dream. Some dreams are just too expensive.

Alrighty, Then, I'll Be a Psychologist

As you might imagine, just about that time I felt very, very lost. Among the many pieces of advice I received from well-meaning friends, someone recommended I take a psychology class. "Hey," I thought, "that might help me, and they could certainly use me as a subject." Taking that class led me to major in psychology with a minor in sociology. "I found it!" I exclaimed. I'd finally found my calling.

I loved psychology and all it had to offer about exploring human behavior—and, even better, exploring me. Graduating with high honors, I landed an internship at a runaway center (lots of kids ran away in the 1970s), then an internship at a hospital adult day-care center (the clients there were way more advanced than me in art). With my credentials and that experience, I felt I was eons ahead of my competition. But all the people I talked to told me there were no jobs in my field unless I had a master's degree. "All the people" and I had a very different opinion about plans for my advanced education.

I often wondered why I wasn't told when I embarked on this career path that I would not get a job in my field unless I had a master's degree and a credential. After graduation, the only job offer I received in the field was as a secretary for a psychotherapist. My big competitive edge over the other candidates was that I knew how to spell the words.

Forget that!

Well, How About HR, Then?

So instead of becoming a bartender—where lots of psych undergraduates end up, because we're good listeners—I ended up in human resources. This is another place where lots of psych undergrads end up, because we are students of human behavior regardless of the milieu. Plus, human resources departments have a lot more in common with bars than you might think. (Notice a drinking theme here?)

I went to work for A.A. No, not *that* A.A! Arthur Andersen and Company. I'd found my calling (again). This seemed like the place where all the action was. I was in business in downtown Chicago at a classy company with many other young professionals. I really felt that I'd finally made it!

What a great place to be a twenty-two-year-old college graduate with visions of being an "up and comer" in the business world. The world of Arthur Anderson was public accounting. In the 1970s that profession was 97 percent male. Picture it...a twenty-two-year-old woman in a 97 percent male dominated business. Yes, it was fun, but I was to realize very soon that the only place I could go in this company was up the ladder in HR...maybe. You see, I wasn't male, and I didn't have the right degree. Sigh.

Don't get me wrong, Arthur Andersen was a great company to work for. They taught me much about business and internal politicking and working with men. I learned about the value of having good relationships with your coworkers, and that honey does indeed catch more bees than vinegar, or whatever that phrase is. All I know is that it works. They also set a high bar for me in learning about professionalism and ethics in business. All in all, A.A. was full of good business sense.

Well, That Dream Lasted for Awhile...

Arthur Andersen did get me to my current home, San Francisco! They transferred me from Chicago, but two years after moving, I came to the realization that my boss wasn't going anywhere soon, and because of that, neither was I. I decided I needed to do a deep-dive into the male world. So I entered the world of engineering at an aerospace company.

I got a job working for what was then Ford Aerospace (now Lockheed). It was the beginning of the equal employment opportunity (EEO) era, where companies had to conscientiously hire women in predominantly male positions, especially if you did business with the government. I was interviewed for a job to serve as a field engineer on a government contract. Lucky me, I was a woman—a good match and good timing. Did I have any experience? No, but I was willing to learn, and I had a great attitude, some of the best qualities one can bring to their work.

I travelled 100 percent of the time in a Ford van with my supervisor. Yes, 100 percent. Our luggage, tools, and electrical wiring were in the back of the van. We travelled to different weather service stations, installing and testing computer rooms and weather tracking computers. I lived like a vagabond on the run for a year, traveling from Portland, Maine, to Tucson, Arizona, and from Anchorage, Alaska, down to San Juan, Puerto Rico.

Hopping from one island to the next in San Juan, I lied about my weight getting on a small commuter plane. When I found out that they weren't just being nosy, that they asked that question to distribute the weight evenly on the plane for safety reasons, I went back to the attendant and confessed that I was actually ten pounds heavier. Ladies, should you ever find yourself in this situation, rest assured that ten pounds doesn't make a difference! The attendant promised me that ten additional pounds on one passenger wouldn't cause the plane to take a spiraling nose dive into the crystal blue waters of the Caribbean Sea. So, now you know.

Eventually I got homesick. I missed coming home to the same place at night, cranking up the stereo, and having a cold tuna fish salad sandwich just the way I like it. Motel 6 doesn't provide this sort of extravagance. On to my next adventure.

Back to Human Resources I Go...NOT!

Returning to San Francisco, I decided I wanted to get a job in human resources again, but I noticed that every job interview I went on included the same question: "Have you ever been responsible for hiring or firing someone?" I had to honestly say "no," and, since this question kept popping up, I obviously had to go out and find work where I could hire and fire people. Sounds a little morbid, but that was my next area for growth.

That led me to my next job, which was working in a company that leased and rented electrical equipment. I interviewed for a job in HR, and again didn't get it. But there was something about me that the people I interviewed with really liked. They brought me back for an interview for a traffic manager position. Not interested. Then they brought me back for an interview for a collections position. Even worse. No way. Finally, they asked if I'd be interested in working in inventory control managing twelve people. "Do I get to hire and fire them?" I asked. "Yup!" they said, and I took the job. This was my big chance. In the end, I worked there for eleven years.

Every two years I thought of leaving the company because I just got bored with the work I was doing. And just about that time, they would promote me or give me some new and interesting work that I could dig into to learn and improve or automate. Over time, I not only managed the Inventory Control Department, but also Purchasing, Traffic (yes, I did learn that in spite of my initial resistance), and Product Management. Eventually, I handled project management of major computer projects, and finally I was promoted to run the Information Services Department. It was a veritable corporate empire! I felt on top of the world. Eleven years working for a successful and growing company that appreciates you will do that for an ambitious person with some talent and a good work ethic. I loved my work there. I was going to be there for a long time. Or so I thought.

Eventually the company was sold to a very large conglomerate. Even though our computer system was determined to be far better than the acquiring company's, they pulled the plug, literally. Closed us down. And I was laid off. Bam!

So, here I was. No job and once again, considering the question, "What do I want to be when I grow up?"

Director of Information Services for the Best Cookie Company in the World!

Well, it really wasn't that obvious or that easy. I actually took about six months off. When would I ever get this opportunity again? Six months after my layoff, almost to the day, I got a call from a friend of mine who asked, "Are you ready to get off your butt and be a productive member of society again?" I told him that I wasn't ready quite yet, but he told me of a cookie and muffin manufacturing company looking for a person to run a major computer conversion. It was too good to pass up, so I said, "I'm just their gal." They thought the same thing and hired me.

Somehow, I had this idea that the food business would be full of women in the higher ranks. I thought I'd finally have some great female role models. Food means lots of women, right? Totally wrong! I was once again swimming in a predominantly male fishpond. Not only that, but the entire IT field at the time only had about 2 percent women in management positions. I had to go out and find my own network of women IT leaders. Well, I did just that, and found my role models in other companies in the same type of work. I wasn't afraid to call these women up and get together to share our plentiful challenges and our occasional successes. We celebrated all of it.

I've Always Wanted to Run My Own Business

We successfully completed a major computer conversion that took two years of long hours and huge learnings. I started to get very excited about "What's next?" until our five-year strategic plan was stopped short by an upcoming reorganization. After three months of being in a holding pattern, and with no date as to when this would change, I was more than bored. I started helping a friend of mine in a business she was just starting. After work hours, I helped her put together some organizational structure and financial guidelines. After about three months we started talking about becoming partners in the business. I didn't know when my IT project was ever going to start up again, so, true to my "any way the wind blows" strategy, I decided that I'd always wanted to run my own business and began working with her.

WBF (We Be Fine!)

We partnered up, and I owned 49 percent of my very own business! It was a wonderful marriage of skills. I brought in my knowledge of operations, finance, and IT, and she was a master at sales and marketing. The plan was that the two of us were going to run the business for five years, create a wildly successful business model, sell it, and become philanthropists.

Well, part of that happened. We worked wonderfully together and grew WBF (we always called it We Be Fine!) into a million dollar business in three years. And then it all went bad. I'm not even sure to this day what happened, but the business and the partnership turned sour. I left the dream behind. The business closed nine months later. The worst part about it was that all of the horrible things you hear about happening when friends go into business together happened to us. I am still sad about it to this day.

Smart Enough to Be a Consultant

Devastated by losing my dream, I took another six-month hiatus before deciding that the next step in my wandering career was to be a consultant. I was sitting outside at lunch one day and gazed down the waterway (I live on an island in a planned community) when I looked up and saw a building about half a mile away from where I live. I set my sights on working there. Since it was so close to home I could avoid all the rush hour commuting, which, quite frankly, makes me cry. About the same time, a friend put me in contact with a consulting group that was searching for someone with my expertise in successfully running large IT projects. You guessed it. Within two weeks, I was working in that building—a dream job of working on Web development (young technology at the time) as a consultant with no overtime and no people reporting to me. Yay!

When Hiring Bonuses Were Too Good to Pass Up

In a short period of time, I proved my worth and my boss liked me...a lot. I was offered a full-time job and the hiring bonus was too good to pass up, so I reentered the arena of full-time employment in Corporate America. Times were good in the dot-com boom period. We had an open budget for the development of my project and some of the best and the brightest working on it. Resources were flowing, and we were well rewarded and recognized for the things we accomplished. Being a habitual achiever, and since recognition was a value of mine at that time, I was at the top of my game. It was fun and the learning opportunities were never-ending. Until the bust, of course, when it was no longer fun, and it all ended rather suddenly.

This Time for Sure...I Know What I Don't Want to Do!

Technology was changing at the speed of a Lamborghini (which is really fast), and I just didn't have the desire to chase after it any longer. Lots of workplace politics went down that gave me a deep understanding of how that game is played, and I left the company knowing I was played out. And if you can't play, you can't be effective.

When I left, I knew I was finished with corporate America. I'd totally had it. The idea of even looking for a job in that arena made me physically nauseous. So I had to stop thinking about it and look for another playground.

Poof! You're a Coach! (What's a Coach?)

At this point, a career consultant advised me, "Pat, you don't have to look for work in the same area you've been in. Be open to work that may never have existed before." Hmmm, good point! When I was in college, running IT organizations wasn't even an option, because that field didn't yet exist. So, I opened up my mind and went to a workshop where the other attendees told me what they thought I should consider—after knowing me for one whole day. Here's the list they came up with:

- A physical fitness or team coach, because I love to cheerlead people on
- One of those people that runs a wilderness course to build leaders, because I like the outdoors
- A job where I can speak to lots of people at once, because I am a good supporter and teacher
- A writer, because I love the written word

There are no big breakthroughs there, but I was intrigued by some of the themes they surfaced. I kept hearing about this field called coaching, and it piqued my interest. It had the elements of cheerleading, building leaders, speaking, and writing. Synchronicity struck again. Within seventy-two hours of finishing that workshop, I signed up to take a coaching fundamentals course. At the time, this was a relatively new field. I took one course and fell in love with this profession, and went on to get my certification in two coaching programs as well as a credential from the International Coach Federation (ICF).

I Think I'll Go Back to Corporate America

I spent my first few years in my own coaching business primarily coaching women in transition who were starting or wanting to grow their own businesses. My initial focus was to get really good at coaching individuals, one on one, to help them find their purpose and their grounding. I wanted to work with individuals and leaders who wanted to play bigger games in their work, community, and even the world. After a few years, I felt the best use of my time was to return to the corporate world as a coach. This individual coaching experience, along with my business background in a variety of functional areas, would be a great combination for coaching people inside organizations in the competencies they most wanted to develop to succeed.

I changed my marketing to orient it more to companies than to individuals. During this time, I received an email that described what I was looking for to a T. The problem was it involved working for a 110-year-old utility company. I knew utility companies were not my style, but the job looked interesting. I kept the email, but went back to evolving my marketing approach. After a few of my friends sent me the very same email, advising me to take a look, I thought I should investigate it further. I figured that if it was a match I could convince them to hire me as a contractor.

Well, they wanted to hire me, but I was not very good at convincing them to make me a contractor—I joined the company less than one month after I sent in my resume. This was certainly a possibility I'd never imagined when I was in college! I was now a leadership coach at California's biggest utility company.

Corporate America Didn't Want Me Back for Long

What an amazing, though brief, ride this gig was. I was hired with almost twenty other coaches to support the leaders of the organization in strengthening their leadership competencies. The company was experiencing a very large and radical business transformation and the intention was to help my clients become better at leading their teams confidently through this transformation.

Perhaps you can imagine the impact I felt when my very first client left the company within two months of our work together. She and I both knew that she was not destined to stay with this company. It was not a match and she was miserable. No one should be miserable day after day in their work. She just needed a bit of coaching to support her decision. We worked together to find a position that more suited and valued her strengths.

For me, it was one of the best work situations I've ever experienced. I was able to work with many emerging and seasoned leaders and guide them along their leadership path, and helped people find work they were truly happy doing. They learned to master their strengths and manage their weaknesses.

I worked with some of the most professional, competent, and heart-based coaches I had ever known. In addition to utilizing my business expertise and coaching training, I was able to open my heart and truly love the people I worked with, both my associates and my clients. It was nearly perfect.

And then...it happened. Our senior executive champion left the company and a new individual was hired. After a few months in the job, this person redistributed our budget, and our department was eliminated. I was laid off faster than you can say Jiminy Cricket.

Life after Corporate Life

So today, as I write this, I am back in my own business, inVisionaria, coaching people in career transitions and leadership competencies. It didn't take me long to fill my life with rewarding and satisfying activities. I work with people to help them find what they love to do in life and how they want to show up as leaders. I support and guide them on the road to making it real.

I'm also working with a group of colleagues to bring to life a new model of coaching. And I am working with another group of women to form a nonprofit called Catalyst Youth Leadership Project. We are committed to creating powerful and affirming experiences of personal leadership for youth that will positively affect the course of their lives and the lives of those they touch. I am also completing a book called *Women Who Play Bigger Games*, or something like that. We'll see what the final title is when the time is right.

Why I'm Telling All of You All of This

For me, this career path has been quite an adventure. I rarely got bored with what I was doing. I'm a lifelong learner, so I was constantly seeking new opportunities where I could keep learning and growing. Quite simply, I am happiest when I'm tossed into something new and I need to learn how to do it. I roll up my sleeves and dig in.

I've often thought that it would be wonderful to have been perfectly clear about my entire career path when I was young—to know exactly what it was I wanted to do and then just do it. But now I realize that this would never have worked for me. After coaching hundreds of people through their own slipping and sliding and shifting and swaying and saving career journeys, I have learned that it doesn't work that way for most of the working world.

My own career path has been like sailing. You never take a straight path to get to where you want to go. You always have to know which way the wind is blowing and adjust your sails. You depend on a higher power that you can't control to fill your sails, and you sail as close to the wind as possible while making headway with sails full and your hair blowing wildly in the wind.

There is always the urge to move forward. Regardless of how tiny the movement is, it's encouraging if at least it is forward.

If you think you've wandered in your career path, take heart! You are not alone.

"What Do You Want to Be When You Grow Up?"

I now know that I will never answer that question—mostly because I now know I never want to grow up.

So, there.

Mai-Huong Le

Business Transformations Extraordinaire

Scrappy Kimberly says: Sometimes it takes me awhile to appreciate how amazing someone is, but this Scrappy woman immediately impressed me as a force of nature. Mai-Huong Le has made a lifetime practice of strengthening herself through a combination of disciplined focus and taking courageous leaps. If you're moving slowly you'll only see this woman's tracks!

My specialty is business transformation. I'm a "Six Sigma Black Belt" with twenty years of experience planning and delivering enterprise-scale applications and solutions across multiple lines of business. I have completed the mergers and acquisitions of over thirty companies, and I have expertise in complex business process integration.

My work has provided me extensive business and systems experience in engineering, IT, financial, and operations environments. I have a successful track record of creating frameworks, strategies, plans, and processes to consistently meet profit and margin targets. My areas of expertise include online services, e-commerce, and business performance management. I have successfully worked with executive management, and effectively use my planning and execution skills to deliver world-class solutions to my partners and customers.

"To succeed, you need to take that gut feeling in what you believe and act on it with all of your heart."
- *Christy Borgeld*

---

4 This Is Your Life—Go For It!

Mai-Huong Le

When you were growing up, how many times did someone tell you to "Keep your eye on the ball"? I have heard it about five hundred thousand times...not that I've been keeping track. Rounding off to the nearest hundred thousand, let's just say too many times...from my teachers, coaches, and teammates. The point of them telling me this, of course, was to get me to focus on the particular task at hand. Over the years, to me that phrase has come to mean, "Keep going for what I want and don't give up." As a result, I was willing to take risks, step out of my comfort zone, and try new experiences. This has made my life a far more interesting adventure than I ever could have imagined as a young child growing up in Asia.

I cannot pinpoint exactly one moment that changed me. I think it was rather a series of moments and circumstances that transformed me into the successful, resilient woman and mother that I am today. I tried new activities, took risks, and persevered through every pursuit. These days I am mentally, emotionally, and physically strong—no longer crying in the heat of every argument, losing debates, or falling ill all the time. I've told my story to many of the young people I mentor, and they are always shocked to hear of the person I once was, which seems a stark contrast to the person I am now. The following are some of the more poignant memories of my journey from being shy, quiet, and timid to becoming an extroverted and confident businessperson, always striving to achieve my goals. It seems that my long and difficult journey actually gave me a gift—the gift of being able to make my dreams a reality. Whatever I set my mind to accomplish, I work extra hard to achieve it, and I do achieve it no matter what.

Protective Roadblocks—Other People Protecting You from Your Own Success

The week I turned sixteen, my sister drove me to apply for my first job at an amusement park. I applied for and received a job in the food concession department. I was not assigned to a particular restaurant or section, but rather was assigned to a backup team. My job was basically to go work in any restaurant or food area that was short of staff on any given day, doing whatever was needed. They couldn't have found a better person than me to do this job since I was a quick learner and able to adapt to new situations rapidly.

After a year of cashiering, serving drinks, making food, waiting on tables, scrubbing grills, and washing floors, I decided that the measly minimum wage I was receiving wasn't enough to make up for the crummy work conditions. I set my sights on the games department. The jobs there seemed to be a lot more fun, there was less dirty work, and employees even received incentive dollars to buy fun merchandise.

When I told my manager that I was going to apply there, she looked at me and, to my surprise, told me that it was very difficult to get into the games department. The interview would be tougher, and I would have to pass an audition. My manager didn't think I was going to make it through the interview. She asked me to stay in the food department working for her. I remember quite clearly my answer to her. I told her that I was going to give it a shot and that I *was* going to make it into the games department.

The next day I got an interview and went to the tryout. Not only did I pass, but I was also given a prize for my audition. My work and social life in the games department was fun, and I received an enormous number of bonus dollars to buy cool merchandise during my career there. Instead of letting my manager limit me to what she thought I was capable of, I believed in myself, took a risk, and got what I wanted. It wouldn't be the last time.

In my first corporate job, I applied for an overseas position. These positions were highly coveted, since they allowed you to work thirty continuous days on then have thirty continuous days off. The company would fly you to the overseas location and fly you back home or anywhere else in the world that you would like to go instead for your thirty-day break. This seemed like a dream come true for me, since I was eager to travel the world.

I told my manager that I would like to apply for one of these positions and asked him to recommend me—part of the bureaucratic process at the time. Several weeks later, I found out that he didn't throw my name into the hat for the job because he was not sure that I would be able to handle an overseas job. He thought it would be best for me to stay in my current role. (Gee, thanks!) He then proceeded to apologize to me for not nominating me. As it turned out, the nominees submitted by other managers were not as qualified as I was. In the midst of his apology, he told me that I was a better developer than the other candidates, and that "I was not the Asian woman he thought I was." You can imagine how uplifted I felt by that remark! Apparently, he had found out earlier that day that I was a black belt who fought at national level competitions, and I had won first place in a Taekwondo competition over the weekend. I think it's safe to say that this new insight into my character transformed his image of me from someone who needed his protection to someone he'd better not get into a bar fight with.

Unfortunately, his revelation came too late for me, and his protectiveness of me cost me a great opportunity. That experience taught me never to assume what people know of me, but instead to always tell them why I'm a good candidate for a job, sharing what experiences I had that would make me successful in a new role. Needless to say, I don't leave my advocates' perceptions of me to chance anymore. I don't go around wearing my Taekwondo outfit at work, but I do make sure they know I can break a board in half with little more than a flick of my finger.

Several years ago, I received an invitation to join a Fortune 500 company. The job description didn't resemble anything that I'd done before. I wouldn't manage any development, test, or operational teams. Instead, I would manage virtual teams of people from various disciplines such as program management, engineering, test, operations, product planning, and customer support. I'd also be supporting an entire suite of online services products and platforms rather than just one.

When I visited my brother the week before starting this new job, he said, "That sounds like a hard job, are you sure you want to do that?" I remember telling him with confidence, "Yes, it will be quite difficult, but I'm prepared to do it." In fact this job was just what I needed! It was a great next step in my professional career. It would allow me to let go of some of my technical skills in engineering and design and focus on my business leadership skills, such as influencing, negotiations, and managing without authority. It would also test my communications skills, as I would be working remotely from my team members.

Ultimately, it turned out to be one of the more challenging and rewarding jobs of my career. This experience gave me the chance to be completely responsible for creating and implementing strategic and tactical plans to beat our global online services delivery competitors. This job also afforded me the visibility to engage with senior executives across various product lines. Looking back, this position was a natural progression for my career, and I'm glad I took the plunge.

Great Mentors—A Mirror in Which to See Myself More Clearly

Humility was a highly desirable characteristic in my culture. People didn't boast about their achievements or talents, and family members would not praise you within earshot. Growing up in this environment was hard on my self-esteem. I heard more reprimands than praise, and my achievements in school were expected not rewarded. I never saw myself as being good at anything. Instead my self-image was that I was rather average, barely meeting my family's expectations. This worked against me in school and work, where communicating your achievements and results is key to success.

Luckily, I always had an abundance of energy and curiosity coupled with a desire to learn new skills and take on new challenges. As a result, I joined clubs, volunteered in organizations, and played on lots of sport teams. I had never been the type of person to sit on the sidelines and watch other people. Nope, not me—I was always an active participant, to say the least. Social clubs and organizations allowed me to meet interesting people, gain different perspectives, and apply my talents. Engaging in sports gave me instant feedback on my performance. The score, as well as my coaches and teammates, let me know immediately how well I was doing, and which areas needed additional practice.

Unfortunately, after years of self-doubt, in spite of all my success, it was still hard for me to see myself as a winner. But I had a good mentor in my Taekwondo instructor. He gave me the positive reinforcement necessary to believe in myself, to push on in my training, to trust in my skills and instincts, and to finally visualize myself as a winner. He told me that I was the #1 fighter in our club, which I found hard to believe as many others outranked me. My instructor reminded me that in order to see myself clearly, I needed to take a step back and view myself from a distance to gauge myself against my opponents and peers from a more objective perspective. His positive influence proved very effective for me. I eventually won many competitions and became the Taekwondo Club President, road manager, and a mentor to many students in our club.

Many years ago, I went to work for a growing software company. It was one of those magical situations where I was in the right place at the right time, and, most significantly, met the right hiring manger. I would eventually work for him off and on at that same company for a total of twelve years. Having proven myself to him in both business and technical areas, he gave me the time and resources to follow through on other opportunities that captured my interest over the years. His support gave me the confidence to continue to look for more interesting opportunities, to further expand my organization's charter, to grow and develop my team and to take on additional challenges outside of my primary area of responsibility. Don't get me wrong: the work was stressful and the hours were long. But I never regretted the mountain of effort it took to accomplish those projects.

One day he came into my office and told me that he'd recommended me for a promotion to senior manager. This took me by surprise, as I'd only been a manager for one year. But he told me I was ready because I had not only done a great job of hiring and building my small team, but had also been a good mentor and coach to two other individuals working in an international office outside of my team. Having his support and belief helped me to develop trust in my own abilities, overcoming years of self-doubt. I received stellar performance reviews and feedback from him. In fact, I sometimes thought that he had more confidence in me than I did myself. That same year I won the "Management Excellence Award" for mentoring and building my team. My employees at the time, whom I still mentor, told me that they really appreciated the way I gave them valuable feedback about their careers, their interpersonal skills, and dealing with challenging work situations. Their feedback was a valuable confirmation of my ability to learn from others and pass on that knowledge to guide others in their journey.

Determination and Perseverance—Stock Up on Plenty of Both

I always set goals for myself—short-term and long-term—whether personal or professional. These goals became the map of my life. They gave me a path and timeline to pursue. It always helps to know where you're going and how long it's going to take to get there. This ensured that I was prepared and packed the right gear. Being a Type A, I love making and having plans and checklists marking my accomplishments. Having these plans and checklists helps make my goals less daunting. It makes them seem more realistic and attainable.

What I didn't realize at the time was that my plans made me more focused. I know what I want, and I know how to get there. Once my route was set, I was more determined than ever to get there, and did so by taking one step at a time. This practice also helps to keep me on track, pushing me through during the hard parts of my journey such as the challenge of balancing a highly successful career and raising my children. Breaking my task into a series of smaller steps allows me to manage my hectic schedule and keeps me sane.

My friends are always amazed by how many things I seem to have going on at the same time. Trust me, juggling that many balls is not easy. Having an updated calendar with reminders definitely helps! Communicating and setting expectations with those around me keeps my world in balance and the balls up in the air. These skills translate well into the business world. Leading high performing teams requires that you give the team a roadmap, responsibilities, resources, and timeline. This way the team stays organized—packed with the correct gear, with roles that are assigned and understood. The team is then able to head in the same direction and arrive at the destination together, all in one piece.

"Let the Game Come to You"

I received this advice from someone I met at a professional association. He was an executive human resources recruiter for a large R&D corporation. I was going through a job transition when I met him, and had recently gone on numerous interviews and met oodles of recruiters. My passion and energy overwhelmed some of my interviewers, while my talents threatened others. He gave me advice on how to channel and control my energy to avoid these unintended negative consequences of my boundless energy and passion. I learned to take deep breaths, speak slower, and put long pauses in my conversations to allow others to process and catch up to my line of thinking. He had a good sense that good things would come my way as a result of my natural talents. "Let it come to you," he said.

This phrase spoke volumes to me, as I tended to be impatient and rush things. I often get stressed out and worried over things I can't control, wishing they'd come faster so I can "get on with it," whatever "it" is. Having the discipline to be well prepared, and training myself to take deep breaths, enabled me to relax and remain calm in challenging situations and with difficult personalities.

A couple of years ago, when I first started working at one of the world's largest software companies, I spoke to a CFO I had worked for many years earlier. He laughed and said, "So, you're going to work for the dark side, huh?" My success depended largely on my ability to influence organizations that did not report to me, or even my division—convincing them to adopt a framework, strategies, and processes to defeat our competition in major markets. As I described the challenges I was facing in this job, he remarked, "It's going to be tough to steer that ship, so be patient. Just do your thing." He had a lot of faith in me, which increased my confidence in engaging with the many execs I needed to interact with in order to gain adoption of our program.

In complex organizations of this size, it is not easy to gain acceptance for such programs, or assurances of resources and funding. I learned to be persistent, persuasive, and flexible. I adapted our framework, molding it to the maturity of the various products and platforms. Learning to be patient came in very handy, since progress was often measured in "glacial" terms and team members were scattered across the globe. The program eventually became highly successful, winning an honorable mention in the annual "Engineering Excellence Awards." And the business results spoke for themselves—significantly increasing revenue as well as the user base for the company.

Follow Your Instinct and Take That Chance

Those six simple words, "Keep your eye on the ball," have helped me achieve so many goals in my professional and personal life. I learned not to take no for an answer, but instead to interpret "no" as meaning "not right now," or "need more clarity," or "it's too complex, simplify it." The power of focus and my drive to accomplish each objective energized me and gave me the strength to forge ahead, confront new challenges, and ultimately succeed. Making plans and reviewing my calendar helps me to mentally and emotionally prepare for the challenge ahead, whether it be a hectic day, a difficult meeting, or a long road trip. Being open to feedback from my coaches, peers, and employees allows me to reassess myself, change my tactics, adjust my game, and win. I'm far from perfect, so there's always room for improvement.

I've never regretted following my instincts and taking a chance, and hope you will learn to trust your instincts, too. Stepping out of your comfort zone and trying something new can produce unexpected surprises. It did for me. It opens new paths, possibilities, and enjoyment that I didn't know existed. I always gear up for the next challenge by telling myself that it won't be easy, but I can do it, so don't give up. My life is much more interesting today due to the many challenges that I undertake. Of course, there's always the next irresistible challenge beckoning to me!

Part II

Wall? What Wall? Oh, You Mean That Pile of Rubble Behind Me?

When I was growing up, girls were supposed to get married and have kids. In high school, I actually won the "Betty Crocker Future Homemaker of America" award, and I even took two years of typing because I thought I might be a secretary before I settled down to raise a family.

Then one day I woke up and found myself in graduate school studying to be a physicist. What??!! While I had loved science all my life (I'd had an Alka-Seltzer-powered rocket when I was a kid, and was the first girl on my street to get a chemistry set), I found that it was more than I could bear to be surrounded by people who thought a calculator on your belt and a pocket protector were fashion statements. In addition, our lab was well past its glory days, and completely unfunded—zip, nada, nothing. As a result, I spent the third year of my graduate studies cleaning garbage out of an enormous laboratory full of the most amazing oddities (I actually found an entire roof from a convertible car in there), ridding the lab of abandoned jars of alkali metals (the kind that explode on contact with water) and refilling disposable ink cartridges for the printer (like I said, there was no funding). This was not the glamorous life of a scientist I'd imagined when I'd read the biography of Marie Curie. Nope! Although I'd had my heart set on getting a Ph.D., which some people claim stands for "Piled Higher and Deeper," I decided it was high time to get a job in the corporate world. M.S. in hand (I'm sure you know what B.S. stands for, and I am pretty sure that M.S. stands for "More of the Same"), I cast my eyes in the direction of full-time gainful employment. My parents were relieved that I was finally going to get a job.

Through a string of lucky coincidences, I landed a job at HP as one of their first female "repairmen," fixing analytical instrumentation like the kind used in environmental testing, drug development, and crime scene investigation. (My theory was that the job offer was due to a mix-up in resumes, but I took it anyway.) It was 1987, and when customers called for help with their HP instrument they were surprised to hear a woman's voice. Sometimes they'd say, "I'd like to speak with someone technical." I'd repaired electronics in the USAF, earned undergraduate degrees in chemistry and physics as well as a master's in physics, so I considered myself pretty technical. I'd assure them that I was the right person to talk to, but if they remained unconvinced I'd politely ask them to hold, wait a few seconds, and then return to the phone using a deeper voice. If that didn't do the trick I'd tell them that the men who used to repair their instruments had met a horrible end, and I was the only one left who could help them. Usually that sufficed.

Being obsessed with doing excellent work, I threw myself into delivering the quality of service that the founders of HP, Bill Hewlett and Dave Packard, would have been proud of. My first year, I was selected as "Rookie of the Year" for the U.S. Midwest region. I still have the leaded crystal decanter to prove it, although I'm afraid to drink anything out of it due to the possible negative health consequences of storing liquor in leaded glassware. Not unlike my work experiences during college, this earned me the admiration of some and the contempt of others. One contemptuous sort spread a vicious rumor that I was sleeping with my boss—a complete lie. (I guess I shouldn't be surprised, though, since on my first day I was warned by one of the more chronologically mature admins that the office staff knew all of the guy's wives, and that they'd be watching me.) Eventually my boss called to ask what I'd done to make people think we'd been sleeping together. At a loss for how to respond to such a moronic question, I finally blurted out: "When the other guys who work for you talk about what an ass you are, I tell them that you've always treated me fairly."

Then I assured him that I wouldn't be saying anything of the sort in the future. Alas, it was clear I'd have to make my fortune somewhere other than mid-America, which simply wasn't ready for an unapologetic wrench-toting repairwoman physicist. So, I transferred to an HP division in Silicon Valley, California, known to midwesterners as "the land of fruits and nuts," where I was almost considered normal.

The HP environment was a poor cultural fit for me, but I stayed for a decade and had six more jobs before giving up entirely on working there. Now, don't take this the wrong way—I'll always be grateful for the opportunities that HP provided me, and I learned enough to fill an entire Wikipedia there. But during that time I quit twice, once out of pure frustration that the company didn't live up to the idealistic reputation described in Tom Peter's *In Search of Excellence: Lessons from America's Best-Run Companies*, and the second time to join one of the exciting Silicon Valley startups that were popping up everywhere. No matter how terrific a company HP was, it just wasn't a match for me. Every year my performance evaluation would include something incendiary like, "Kimberly has unrealistically high expectations of herself and others." I'd retort, "Hey, those aren't *my* expectations, buddy! Those are the expectations of the founders of this company, Bill and Dave, and I think we owe it to them to live up to their fine legacy!"

Although HP made good use of my ability to achieve impossible results, HP didn't agree with my assessment of my leadership potential. After a decade, I was still just a first-level manager with no prospects for rising in the ranks, and the company showed no signs of following my advice to transform into the kind of place I'd love to work. Fortunately for me, a wonderful mentor spotted what a misfit I was and sponsored my work with an executive coach who flatly told me, "Kimberly, what the hell are you doing at HP?! You're an ENFP in a sea of 80 percent ISTJs (Myers-Briggs speak for "you don't fit in"), and as such you're not just different—you're wrong. You must feel like a fish swimming upstream all day long." She sure was right about that! She also mentioned to me that when ISTJs (typical analytical types) talk with ENFPs (lively, emotional, expressive types) they feel as though they're talking to a blowtorch. I tried arguing that Lew Platt, one of HP's CEOs during my tenure, was an ENFP, but she reminded me that:

1. he was a man, and
2. he had protection.

OK, I get it! After ten years of doing everything I could to make it work, this sealed it. Shattered hopes in hand, I left muttering something about writing a book titled *In Search of Excrement: The Crap that REALLY Happens at HP.*

Much to my delight, the startups I joined were teeming with other Scrappy women like me and those who wrote this section—smart, well-educated, witty individuals who can lead a project, design a product launch plan, calculate an algebraic equation, and choose the perfect scarf to go with an outfit, all while doing thirty minutes on a stationary bicycle. I had finally found my tribe! Wahoo! At long last I was not the most intense, most assertive, or most capable woman I knew. "El reliefo!" This was a lot more fun than squeezing myself into a constrictive norm and being "appropriately subordinate," as I'd been advised to be in order to be tolerated at HP.

As you read about Carole, Eldette, and Terrie, you'll understand why I invited them to share their stories in this book. These women look at obstacles the way Godzilla looks at a bus he's about to eat. (Godzilla didn't have anything against the people in the bus, mind you. He just happened to wreak destruction in his path on his way somewhere he was in a big fat hurry to get to.) Not that I'd want to take this analogy too much farther, but take my word for it—you don't want to be standing between these Scrappy Businesswomen™ and their goals. You might just end up digging yourself out of a pile of rubble as you watch them vanish into the distance, the tattered remains of your backside trailing behind them.

Lean back and learn from women who do what everyone else says can't be done!

- Scrappy Kimberly

"You can't build a reputation on what you are going to do."
- *Henry Ford*

Carole Amos

**Global Channel Marketing Director,
Ironkey, Inc.**

Scrappy Kimberly says: What's my favorite
Scrappy trait possessed by Carole Amos? She's
got a razor-sharp wit and the courage to use it!
Sure, lots of people think of clever things to say
a couple of hours after an opportunity presents
itself. But Carole is one of those gifted people
who can see the preposterousness of a situation
real-time, and provide insightful commentary that
dispels the foggy thinking typical of mere
mortals. Illusions vanish as she says what others
only dare to think.

I love working with high-tech products. There's nothing more fun than helping a product develop out of an idea to become a real-life problem solver for customers. Spanning the techies and intuitive types, from engineers to salespeople and everyone in between, is delightful. My first career was software engineering; the second, product marketing. After a few years as a consultant, I am now developing sales channels for my clients.

I believe that successful businesses are made through early customer feedback, and that iterative processes are the most efficient. Your business plan never survives your first engagement with your customer. You may think you know what the customer needs, wants, and will do with your product, but you are likely to be surprised by what they think when you get out and talk with them. Many products veer from their original plan once their creators engage with prospective customers.

I believe that customer feedback, early and often, is crucial for success.

"Life is a banquet, and most poor suckers are starving to death."
- *Rosalind Russell*

Chapter

5 Disappearing the "Wall of No"

Carole Amos

Have you ever noticed that chasing your dreams just makes them retreat? Sometimes stalking them creates the opposite of the result we're seeking. But, just like that proverbial butterfly, happiness will frequently land on your shoulder while you're otherwise occupied.

The past couple of years have been like that for me. One day recently, I was hanging out in my "vacation" home in Rochester, New York, wondering what it means to be Scrappy. (My friend Kimberly Wiefling seemed to think I was, and I was warming up to the idea.) I was there for a few days of vacation and family visits before heading back to Silicon Valley, my new home, and a return to work. It was late June, and summer had finally bloomed in this part of the world. The weather was absolutely beautiful, and I was so tickled to be there that I could barely contain my sighs of contentment.

While visiting with a friend, I mentioned the Scrappy Businesswomen™ project. As I wondered aloud what I'd write, my friend Tanya piped up, "Well, my friend, three years ago you moved back to Rochester in the midst of getting divorced while your mom was dying. Back then, you said your ideal life would be one foot in

Europe, one foot in Rochester, and one foot on the West Coast. (OK, that's three feet, but never mind.) Now look at you!" Suddenly, I realized that my ideal life was taking shape before my very eyes. I currently have a great job at an exciting, fun startup in Los Altos, California. I bought a townhouse in nearby Mountain View in February, while keeping the New York house near my family in Rochester. And I have good friends in Germany and the UK that I visit occasionally. This *is* my beautiful life. How did I get here? It seemed to all appear while I wasn't paying attention. How did I do that? It turns out, I was Scrappy through and through.

You'll Put Your Eye Out!

A lot of people along the way told me what I shouldn't or couldn't do, starting with how I shouldn't consider a career in engineering. Maybe they were just kidding around with me, but this was the 1970s, and I took it seriously. "Girls can't be engineers!" exclaimed one family friend. This prompted an immediate response of, "Ohkaaay...that's precisely what I'll do then!" There were six women in our university class of 120 electrical engineering students. The guys treated us as if we were from another planet—possibly friendly, but they'd seen the movie *Aliens*. Best not get too close, just in case we intended to use their bodies as hosts for some creature that might pop right through their chests in the middle of an exam. The professors were evenhanded. One was a jerk to everyone equally. As for the rest, there was no evidence of any repressive sexism, at least none that I was aware of. Maybe I was just too young and naïve to notice, but none of the other women seemed to have any problems, so I'm at least living under the illusion that there just weren't any.

Walking Among Dinosaurs

My first real job out of college was at GE Aerospace and Electronics Systems Division (AESD). I was hired into the QA group, courtesy of GE's focus on diversity. Court-mandated focus, I believe—thank you, very much. I learned a lot on that job. GE AESD in the early '80s was a weird space-time coordinate to inhabit. The '70s had been a hard time for the aerospace industry, and they had laid off a lot of people, mostly their junior people. In the early '80s, as business picked up, they started hiring right out of college, so there were a hundred or so college grads in their early twenties working with a bunch of men in their forties and fifties. This bimodal population of employees was more than a little awkward in this extremely conservative industry in this tiny little industrial town in upstate New York. The attitude in the QA group was very much like that I'd encountered during my summer work at Delco while I was in college: "Just do yer job. Of course you hate the company and the bosses, but you'll work all yer life here until you retire, then die pretty quickly because you're not useful anymore. Don't cause a fuss. Don't speak up. And don't work too hard—you'll make the rest of us look bad."

Bleeeaaach!!! Welcome to my nightmare! It seemed like I was walking among dinosaurs. The attitude was defeatist, pessimistic, grim, and drained the life right out of any living creature that tried to cross through this "Wall of No." I wanted no part of it. (And this was before I'd been exposed to anything like the Law of Attraction or the most current quantum physics theories on so-called reality.) So, in spite of being told by one such psychic vampire, "You can't move into the software group out of QA!" I interviewed for a position in the software group and got it. Of course, the QA group expected me to turn it down because it just wasn't done—to move out or move up, that is. Hah! Out I went like a shot! *Scrappy can mean resisting the prevailing attitude.* And resist I did.

Make "The Man" Work For You

My best friend had also gotten a job at GE around the same time, and we helped each other through a lot of this as women do—talking about the situations we encountered, brainstorming solutions. (And sometimes fantasizing about taking over and sending them all to the tar pits where they belonged. Well, at least I fantasized that!)

One old goat thought that she was just lovely. Well, he was right in that. He started leaving her notes, comparing himself to a puppy who would be so excited that he'd piddle if she'd pet him. Eeeew, gross! Can't imagine what he was thinking. I mean, does anybody find that attractive?! We dithered a bit about what to do—but then heard he'd done the same to other women. She went to management and shared his canine fantasies with the corporate dogcatcher. It turns out that she was the first one to do so. He might have piddled, but for entirely different reasons than his love notes indicated. He wouldn't look her in the eye after his talk with the boss.

Another guy wouldn't stop smoking in the lab. (Yes, people actually did smoke inside the normal work area once upon a time.) We figured we wouldn't get anywhere complaining about our lungs, so we complained this was causing the computer to crash. (No, really, it can happen! Smoke particles are bigger than the gap for the disk drive head.) That did the trick. *Scrappy can mean getting the current system to work for you.*

Don't You Dare, Little Missy!

"You can't just pick up and move across country!" was the next Wall of No that someone attempted to construct in my path. This one was easier, as by then I was married, and bold decisions seem easier when two people agree to take the plunge together. *Scrappy can mean enlisting allies and partners and a circle of advisors*, to help you sort through all the possibilities this life offers or push through the Wall of No that you sometimes encounter.

That's Just Not Done!

Over the next few years, I got a bushel of resistance from family as I stretched and grew and changed jobs, Silicon Valley style. As I mentioned, they were used to someone getting a job—one job—and staying with it for their entire life no matter how detestable the job. Not surprisingly, they just didn't understand the entrepreneurial environment and the sometimes frenetic pace of "The Valley," as we call it. It seemed to me that I would get the best out of a job within a couple years then start longing for new challenges, or at least new scenery. Most of the places I worked were pretty small, and a couple were zombie companies—businesses based on a good idea that never gained traction or grew, but were just destined to keep shambling on. Once I'd mastered the job, there was nothing new to learn or do. I was spending about two years per company, but I certainly did not want to end up with a thirty-year career consisting of two years of experience repeated fifteen times, especially when I was bobbing around in a sea of fresh ideas, exciting companies, and mind-expanding experiences! So I pretty much ignored the exhortations of my family and occasionally hopped, skipped, and jumped from job to job in the style common to this innovative culture. *Scrappy can mean making up your own mind, and being OK if no one else sees your point of view.*

Send in the Clones!

Next, I found myself immersed in the whirlwind of a very successful job at Sun Microsystems, this time for five years—practically a "lifer" in this environment. The company and I were growing like crazy, right along with the whole dot-com boom. There was so much work, I would have had to have been an octopus or cloned myself to get it all done.

Being part of the Java group at Sun was exciting, tremendously satisfying, and positively exhausting. This is where I learned that you do need to toot your own horn, highlight what you're doing, and promote yourself in order to succeed in the professional world. If you don't, you and your contributions get lost in the mayhem. This was also when I learned that I was the one who needed to decide when I'd done enough for the day, for the week, on a project. No one was ever going to burst into my office, insist that I'd done plenty of work, and send me home to a good night's rest. That lesson hit home when paramedics carried out a couple of people on stretchers over the course of two years, after they collapsed at their desks from the twenty-hour workdays. (There's a reason they call some projects "death marches.") *Scrappy can mean taking care of yourself—no one else can do that for you!*

Make Mine a Bubbly

"Go out on your own? Work for yourself? Are you crazy? There's no security in that!" This was the next form the wall took. By early 2000, I had a whole Scrappy team of advisors, aka gal pals, who were exploring different ways to earn a living besides the salaried job grind. The boldest—our intrepid explorer and editor Kimberly Wiefling—would exhort me to "Jump! Make the water up on the way down!"—something she'd learned from one of her mentors over the years. She had decided to work for herself, and, in Nike-shoe fashion, just did it. She claimed that all it took to start a business was printing up some business cards and spreading the rumor that you were in business, so I took a deep breath and jumped, following her inspiring lead. Yup, I quit my job, took a couple weeks off, got a business license, cobbled together a website, and had business cards printed up. Voila! I'm a consultant! The sense of freedom was like swimming in champagne. My attitude changed—I had grown tired of the restrictions placed on me by the geological layers of bosses at company after company. As a consultant, outside of the corporate hierarchy, my knowledge and contributions were taken as expert wisdom. How refreshing! *Scrappy can mean making up your own path and permitting yourself to explore.*

How Can We Open Their Minds?

Consulting with one of the dot-com startups was especially fun. A group of Ph.D.s created a company through a spin out of a research lab. Their goal was to make the whole Web surfing experience more personalized. Instead of getting millions of responses to a search query, the surf-along technology would personalize search results for you. If I searched for "java," it magically knew I was looking for the coffee, not the island or the programming language.

It was great fun being involved near the beginning of the company, helping to shape it and the product. It quickly became clear that the brilliant founders and extremely talented lead engineers had no idea how to perceive what they had created from the eyes of a typical user, which is why they needed my expertise. The typical user was a novice to moderately-skilled computer user who had been using Internet search for only a few months, not a Ph.D. in linguistic expression or information retrieval like these guys.

When I joined the team, the product required deep technical knowledge about the way it was built in order to make sense to the user. This was not going to attract the mass-market adoption that we wanted. To get the engineering team the information they needed about the usability of the product, I pulled together "friends and family" usability testing—recruiting more typical end users from people referred to us by the employees. We did the testing at the office; no fancy, expensive, third-party set-up requiring separate rooms, one-way glass, and tons of cash—just the tester, a list of tasks we'd like them to perform, and the engineers sitting quietly behind them, watching as they tried to use the product.

Oh, it was sweet to see the light dawn on the faces of the engineers as the testers struggled to understand the user interface, and attempted to use the product in ways they could never have foreseen. These representatives of potential clients had difficulty doing the simplest things. This campaign inspired a focus on the usability of the product, and we even hired a usability specialist to assure that it was easy to learn and easy to use. To help keep that in their minds, I made a collage of typical users from pictures out of magazines, and sometimes would lead a chant: "We are not our target customer!" *Scrappy can mean finding creative ways to make your point and help the team succeed.*

Buddy, Can You Spare $150K?

Another startup from that era began life as a successful consumer credit marketplace. You could apply online and, behind the scenes, banks would score your information and decide whether to extend credit or make a loan. Customer acquisition costs were high, however, and as the year 2000 did a nosedive into recession, the CEO decided that he wanted to recast the product into a credit-scoring hosted service for enterprises. Great idea. But the remaining team was mostly from consumer products companies, so I was brought in due to my enterprise experience.

Once again, the toughest thing to do was to educate the team on their target customer. They started out making a product to help automate a credit department that they hallucinated would sell for $150,000 plus a customization fee. How much can a credit manager sign for? Typically, around $5,000. Oops! I educated them on a sales process that starts with the department manager, has to go up to IT, over to a mid-level financial controller, then to the CFO. This is way different than selling burgers at a roadside fast food joint. They also initially expected that prospective customers would be easy to find, and we'd be able to sell for full price as soon as the product was ready. A nice fantasy, but...not a chance! They'd moved into an area where buyers are conservative and need lots of proof points first, and a key proof point is a reference customer—someone who's already using the product and delighted with it.

I could tell that my message wasn't getting through, so I bought a copy of *Crossing the Chasm* for the CTO. He read it and I got another one of those great face-lighting moments as illumination descended upon him and he finally understood what we had to do to go to market. As a result, he and I teamed up to educate the rest of the team. *Scrappy can mean enlisting the help of outside expertise to make a crucial point.*

In 2008, I took a job that challenges all my Scrappy skills at a very fast-growing startup. This time I have taken on challenges and delivered on projects unlike anything I have done before—at lightning speed. It's absolutely thrilling and so much fun. At this point in my life, any resistance or Wall of No that I face is primarily generated by me. My family now admires what I've done, rather than cautioning me on my choices. So many friends and former coworkers have also started their own businesses—whether a sole proprietorship or a venture-funded startup. As a result, I've surrounded myself with people who believe in creating their own lives and agree that the life they get is largely a result of their behaviors and attitudes. Boundaries that I encounter now are my own internal limitations, and I have some well-proven techniques for overcoming such self-induced limitations, some of which I've shared with you here. *Scrappy can mean understanding yourself well enough to catch one of those self-limiting beliefs as they fly through your brain, and dismiss it as just a thought, not the truth.*

All told, I have not acted, or even felt, Scrappy all the time. I have sometimes agonized, or waffled, or dragged myself kicking and screaming through a change. But looking back at what I've done, what I've been through, what I've accomplished, I'm proud of myself. And that, my friends, may be the Scrappiest achievement of all.

Eldette Davie

Ms. "You Say I Can't Do What?"

Scrappy Kimberly says: Maybe it sounds a bit "last century," but I'm not one to make friends with people I've never met in person. Eldette is a rare exception. She's a project manager from Africa, a mysterious continent that has always intrigued me. We first connected through my Scrappy Project Management book and our commiseration over the thanklessness of the project management profession. (I'm truly hoping that she's a real person, and not an ebony-colored Labrador retriever posing as a human.) Every time I receive an email from Eldette I feel her Scrappiness leaping from the screen. Her matter-of-fact approach to overcoming one insurmountable obstacle after another, like some tireless runner leaping giant logs across her path, make her an inspiration to me, and thoroughly qualified for the Scrappy Businesswoman's Hall of Fame. (That, and the fact that she's petted a lion.)

After graduating with a diploma in marketing, I joined a computer company and found what I liked doing most—being around computers. My sins include time in blue chip companies, "Big 5" consulting houses, and work in presales and business consulting in Europe and Africa.

I thrive on learning new things, and I'm intrigued by metaphysics and the concept of world connectedness. I am passionate about all things outdoorsy—photography, sport (the more extreme the better), my family (especially my four-footed children), and music you can listen to without going deaf. I dislike more than words could express: injustice, dishonesty, thoughtlessness, and prejudice.

At the moment, I'm a program manager for the largest technology-only consulting house in South Africa, working on a project that is making me go grey. (As a result, I dye my hair!) I can't tell you how valuable Scrappiness has been in my life, never more than in my current challenges.

"Regrets are a waste of time. They're the past crippling you in the present."
- *Federico Fellini,* from the movie *Under the Tuscan Sun*

---

6 What Was I Thinking?

Eldette Davie

I live in Africa, but not in a mud hut as many people unfamiliar with Africa might imagine. I don't have elephants or lions running around my garden. We have electricity and inflation, drive cars in traffic jams, and pay exorbitant amounts for petrol (gas, as you might call it elsewhere). All in all, as exotic as Africa sounds to some people, it's pretty routine stuff.

We usually don't have projects like the one I'm currently working on (and going to tell you the story of in this chapter), but this one takes the cake and is worth a rant. (It's less costly than therapy!) But *please* don't get the idea this is the norm in Africa, OK? This continent is too diverse to be summed up in anything as brief as a single chapter of a book anyway. I hope you'll get some sense of my Scrappy business world by taking this journey through one project from hell that summarizes so much of the worst and best of my business life experience.

White "African" Cruella De Vil

After graduating at the age of eighteen in 1979 from a snobby, academic, all girls' high school in my native South Africa, I longed to study to become a lawyer. My Scottish father forbade it! According to him, I needed to go into the army and learn proper discipline, and he thought I was well suited for this career as I had (and still have!) a voice like a sergeant major. He thought I'd be well served to go and study computers or engineering after that. Thanks, Dad.

Naturally, I was determined not to follow his advice. But a little research surfaced the fact that I was, apparently, *already* too liberal to be an attorney. I realized that studying law would most likely lead me directly to being locked up *in* jail rather than keeping anyone out of it. Besides, I was told, "You are deeply misguided about what law is really about!"

On to the army. I walk with military purpose (not a catwalk model's prance, to be sure), and have never been regarded as a shy, retiring person, so I would probably have fit into the army. I have the personality for it, too. In fact, I've heard people say they would rather drop a heavy lead weight from a dizzying height onto their foot than confront me; my projected confidence level is rather high. But I was still determined not to listen to my dear old dad. So to punish him (yep, daft thoughts!), I went to work at a butchery with fancy, up-market deli outlets. (I can carve a mean roast!)

Carving meat wasn't all it was cracked up to be. Although I'd taken the deli job to get back at my dad, I resigned soon after to leave South Africa and travel through Europe because I realized that I was the only one suffering! For many months I lived in trains and train stations, worked as a domestic maid, became a companion to a dear, wise old lady, and briefly held other enterprising jobs—hoping my father would relent (he didn't).

After I returned home, my remarkable mom negotiated a deal with my dad where I could attend a particularly conservative university studying in Afrikaans (my second language, a Dutch/German derivative) for a degree in commerce, an activity that lasted all of one year. At the end of the year we—the university and I, that is—realized we were not of similar mindsets, so I transferred to a technical university and completed a marketing diploma instead.

During my three years of marketing study, I worked as a flambé waitress and cooked yummy food at the guests' tables (can still prepare mouth watering meals, *as well as* carving a roast), and doubled as a barman (I know when you've had too much to drink, even if you don't!)—basically, anything legal that paid my bills.

After graduation, I joined a computer company in a marketing role and found my passion—computers. I've never stopped learning, experimenting, and growing since. In the twenty-five years I've been in the IT industry, I have built servers and networks, designed and tested applications, and consulted—all of this in a variety of niche markets. I have also done loads of application implementations and ERP suites in a number of vertical markets throughout Africa. I never explicitly *studied* computers, but because this interested me, I've spent twenty-five years learning on the job and late at night with the hounds of hell chomping at my butt. I've enjoyed every moment of this because it was so darn *fascinating and intriguing.*

Have you ever been in a situation where someone tells you a story or relates an anecdote and you think, wow I've been there? Kind of comforting when you hear someone else has done the *silly*, or been ill-treated (or whatever else you may be feeling), and survived!

Men don't seem to think this way, but I find that women often do! We are comforted when we hear that someone else has walked the fire walk and survived. (I've actually done a fire walk!) Well, this challenge has every single component of what should not happen in business or a project, so I'll tell you the story of who I am through this one project. What I've learned through my experience may help you survive whatever impossible challenge you're currently up against.

Something Smells Fishy

Picture this. Its 8:10 a.m., and a daybreak Steering Committee meeting has just finished. (Why are they scheduled then? Do you suppose we think better at that time of day?) The client had postponed our project, as they needed to finalize some emergent legal matters—an anticipated three-month break. "Oh well, that was that!" I thought.

My company bigwigs called me aside, and told me that they had an interesting "challenge." Was I up for it? I pointed out I currently *had* an interesting challenge since there were outstanding issues on the project regardless of the requested break. Besides what type of question is that, *"Was I up for a challenge?"* I did a bungee jump off the highest bridge in the Southern Hemisphere when it was still a novelty. I don't scare, see? Challenge, what a cheek!

My grandmother, whom I'd loved with all my being, had very recently passed away, and it felt as though my heart had broken beyond ever being fixable. The iron maiden had a sore heart. I was walking straight and tall but my inner being felt torn apart, and I thought this challenge might take my mind off the aching hole. Plus, aren't we all validated by our work? Isn't our self-worth measured by the recognition we are given at work? Isn't our value as a human being measured by the achievements we are acknowledged for? Without that we could be personally invalidated, right?

Are you nodding your head as you read, or is it just me? Aren't we women dim sometimes! I mean, what shade of stupid was I acting out of?!

The skinny on this project was that if I tied up a few loose ends, I would deliver the go-live in three months, proving that experienced project managers could resuscitate the dead, deliver on time, and be back on their own project after the delay. True story! A recording of a voice kept running through my head saying, "Nothing can go wrong, go wrong, go wrong, go wrong...." I should have taken the first bus out of town!

Yup, There's Definitely a Stench in Here

Being the well-trained skeptic that surviving project managers become, I asked the relevant questions. The first warning sign was that two different business units needed to deliver as one, but inter-business-unit disagreements and finger pointing complicated the final delivery. This was no small matter, as a substantial amount of money was outstanding, which would be paid on delivery. I started to imagine tinkling bells, fairy dust, and laughter as they continued to describe the glowing prospects for success with me at the helm.

The whole scene made me recall my presales days, when life was fun and I used to fly around Paris, Poland, and Prague peddling the same violin tunes being heaped upon me. In those days, my acumen, quick wit, and public speaking abilities were my preferred weapons of trade. The company I worked for then had a mantra that guided us: "Be economical with the truth." I didn't like it then, and I sure didn't like being on the receiving end of this kind of babble now. The trouble with economies of truth, however, is that it is often awhile before one understands how extremely economically the truth has been shared. I fell for it.

The reason I was chosen, they told me, was ____ (insert any sparkly nice words and compliments that come to mind). Because I was so ___, I would rapidly understand the bridging requirements. Ladies, this is what we do for and to ourselves; we are enticed when people are nice to us, we are won over when we are praised, and we feel joyful at being able to prove how good we are. Well, maybe that's just me but, geez Louise, I heard violins and harps, got my ego stroked, and was sucked right in!

I joined three days later to find a team that wasn't a *team* at all—different groups sitting in totally different areas. Nope, this was no team. We were starting from scratch on this one. In early client discussions, it became clear they would burn me at the stake in the event of failure if they could get away without legal prosecution. They might even be willing to risk a manslaughter conviction. This was a war zone.

I made the following "Scrappy Notes to Self" (NTS) at the time:

Priority 1 - *Restore client-favorable relationship, even if that means eating humble pie or making yourself available for near-naked public flogging. If the latter, make sure you're wearing good underwear.*

Priority 2 - *Introduce a sense of one team, no matter how much personal money is required to purchase the beer and bowling games.*

Priority 3 - *Everything else. (That included many typical project activities that I had not yet observed, and appeared to be missing.)*

Naturally, I had a little chat with my PMO director, who admitted they had some "challenges" but assured me of their undying faith in my ability to get the job done, and I was caught again by the fluffy words. I am still toying with the idea of whether to take a contract out on his life, but I can't completely blame him since I can't quite figure out what he actually knew at that point.

Personally, I believe in a "can do" work ethic, and that people will rise to the occasion if you put a worthy challenge before them. I am also fascinated by all things quantum and metaphysical, and somehow persuaded myself that this challenge had crossed my path because it was an experience that I desperately needed in order to fulfill my own destiny. Oh, did I mention that I also believe in the tooth fairy? Looking back, it's clear that I essentially bushwhacked myself into this "911—Nurse! Nurse! I feel worse!" project as a result of my own ego and the somewhat strange paradigm I have for interpreting what crosses my life path.

Oh, Dear Gawd, There's a Reason It Smells So Awful!

On I lurched. I requested the project documentation. What a load of hot unadulterated balderdash that was! There were no conventions, procedures, or standards, and the words in the documents were meaningless. My request for specification documents was greeted with gusty laughter—there were none! The project had changed too quickly and too much to establish a single version of the truth. Each time someone attempted this feat, the scope had changed dramatically before the ink was dry, so they had given up.

I realized team members might have their own documentation, so I asked them what was up, shot the breeze, sought to understand their roles, and posed my prime question: "What is your one silver bullet, i.e., what does this project need most right now? Oh, and please may I have your documentation?" I collected many and different bullets—silver, brass, and plain rusty iron (along with some handguns and surface-to-air missiles), adding more rubble to the pile on my desk.

I asked for any contractual detail. None. We had no idea what we were aiming at. Holy canola, how so? At this point, there was some mumbling about how all of the original consultants had resigned and left the company. The puzzle pieces were starting to fall into place, and I began to understand why we were at the place where we were.

This project hadn't started off as a stinking pile of failure ready to leap onto the next unwary PM who happened to walk by. It happens that the initial contract was written by a world-renowned consulting house specializing in business consulting, but they had no intention of delivering their recommended IT solution themselves! Our company had agreed to implement on someone else's project recommendation (big mistake!), and this had transformed into a hydra. Because our company desperately wanted to retain the deal, they had agreed to continue without contesting any changes! I asked what they had been thinking. "Protecting our source of revenue," I was told. Well, that has proved to be a very expensive miscalculation!

Undoubtedly, the PMs among readers will realize that one question is blindingly obvious: if there is no formally agreed scoping document, functional specification, or contract, how on this green earth do we know what the client is expecting or whether we have done it to get paid? Asking this question just resulted in more laughter, which seemed less funny to me every minute. People shook their heads while muttering. "Why do you think we are where we are?" they asked me. "Don't ask us, we just work here!" Have you ever discovered that you've been unknowingly walking around with a target on your back and a red laser spot from a sniper's rifle dancing merrily across it?

It's Tough to Do Your Job While Holding Your Nose

I just couldn't believe this. Without proper guidance, control, or management, the consulting team had been bullied into agreeing to do whatever had been requested of them. And the requests had rolled in. In fact, one senior person had said, I quote, "You dream it, and we build it." Which la-la-land had this fool come from? Had nobody ever learned how to use a handy little word familiar to every toddler—*no*? They told me they needed to please the client, which meant they couldn't say the "N" word. Houston, we have a problem! How bloody well pleased do they look now? Riddle me that, Batman!

I asked how they knew they were ready to go live given the current state of affairs. Turns out that was an easy question to answer. The directors had told them to go live or else. What a frightfully compelling reason! Threaten exhausted, demoralized staff to set a *firm date* in the sand, a date impossible to achieve, while at the same time raising client expectations once more. Then crucify the staff when they don't deliver miracles. What a simply brilliant plan: horse, carrot, whip, Valium, Prozac! That's akin to setting a time limit on open heart surgery and telling the surgeon to stitch up the patient when time's up no matter how far along the operation is. That process wouldn't bode well for the patient, and it doesn't work for complicated software projects, either.

So, the client **hated** us, did not trust one person on our project, and none of us actually knew for a certainty what we were supposed to be doing, or whether we had actually done *it* all, or even part of *it*. No wonder this project was terminally sick.

Hell would freeze over solidly, hundreds of meters deep in the most arid desert and within nanoseconds, if we delivered even a partial solution on the due date. Quite simply—not gonna happen.

Help Me Drag This Stinking Carcass Outta Here, Would Ya?!

I went back to my PMO director and told him the project real deal—that it was sheer madness, the hallucinations of a madman. He confessed that this project was the final straw for our company, and the very reason he had been instructed to set up an enterprise-wide PMO office. There had been too many contentious projects and consequences. We had to clean up our processes (no kidding), and mentor and coach people into the right way to do this work. The PMO dream would conk in and be dead if we did not rescue this deal, so we first had to deliver this project. Ah, there's the rub!

Although he had heard reports on the project, it was inconceivable to him that a project could be this broken. But he felt that if anyone could help, it would be me. My lucky day, why do women pick this bait up so quickly, why? Men at that point turn around, call horse scheize for what it is, and walk away without fear of retribution or being called weak. Women go gooey and try to deliver the impossible! Anyhow, the most critical instruction was that we had to somehow drag the stinking carcass of this project over the line, no matter what, so we could get paid.

I went home, had the greater portion of a good bottle of red wine, played with my puppy Max, and chatted with my three cats. My pets were welcome company, since my partner was not talking to me as a consequence of the solid fourteen days of long, late nights at the office. My furry friends all agreed with me though: I was insane! "My human mother is an overachiever with a never-give-up attitude, bless her heart." I firmly believe there are times when it takes more guts and character to relinquish and say we have to go back to before it was so broken, whatever it takes and whoever it upsets.

The next morning I walked in and announced to the team that we were going to plan! Of course their response was, *"Isn't that your job? Don't you PM types do that? We just deliver the goods."* Well, fat lot of good they had been at doing that. So we planned, we yelled at each other, fingers got pointed all around, there was wailing, then more wailing, doors banged, and a few people stormed out. Some threatened to leave permanently, and no one rose to stop them, least of all me. When in doubt, go back to planning; you will at least know what the picture looks like.

With the searching questions and provisional planning finished, we established there was a hole the size of China in our solution, and that we didn't possess the expertise or quantity of people to fix this hole within twelve months, let alone three.

The Big Shots didn't want to hear that, told me I was mad, that I was signing the unit's death warrant. The client had stopped paying because we had failed so many times, and we were already millions over budget. We'd get a big chunk of cash after the first month up and running successfully, but we had to go live *now*. Well, I'm not a liar, so I just couldn't tell them what they wanted to hear, no matter how badly they wanted to hear it.

We needed a way to deliver bad news—really bad news. In my experience, I've found it works best to be quite devoid of emotion and state the facts sequentially, logically, and rationally in bullet format, in a respectful but unstressed, matter-of-fact tone. (You might want to use this technique the next time you quit your job or leave your boyfriend.)

Once the weight of the bad news has settled in there is inevitably a tsunami of emotional debris, which you just have to let wash right over you until the other party calms down, if they calm down. If they don't calm down, well, make sure you are standing nearest the door. The next wave is the finger pointing and blame game. During that phase, it's best to acknowledge quite unreservedly that mistakes had been made on all sides, offer no excuses, but focus on the future. In our case, we needed to state what our plans were to make it right, and how we would ensure that we stayed on the right path.

I wanted to deliver this message myself, but the idea was that a bigwig carried more weight and authority! He was less than thrilled. Reluctantly, he announced that we would not deliver on the expected date, and that the actual date was quite a bit later. Only, to my surprise, he didn't give the date we agreed to. Instead, he promised something less preposterous but still unattainable except through wishing, hoping, and miracles. Here we go, again!

The Aroma Begins to Lift

Well, somehow we got through the tsunami, the debris, finger-pointing and blaming aftermath, and yet another pie-in-the-sky promise. Of all the oddball dysfunctional and incompetent behavior I've witnessed in my life, this particular project has had it all! If I hadn't seen it for myself, I would never have believed a project could be so derailed.

We're finally seeing the smoke clear, and I've glimpsed a shred of daylight here and there as we've untangled our biggest challenges. We will not make the new deadline date, but I have made it clear that I will work hammer and tongs to get this sorted ASAP. I won't consider myself a failure unless I miss the realistic date based on thoughtful consideration, not blind hope.

As I write this cathartic tale, I'm relishing the thought that our first full unit testing just finished, and we're actually deploying the first fully testable version of this software tonight. Although at one point it seemed impossible, at the time of this writing we look set for reaching the first planned milestone in over *three years*. That's how it is with impossible tasks. They just take a bit of working at, and fair quantities of something called Rescue Remedy. (Tastes like a martini—bought at any health store, promotes deep relaxation!)

The team has been transported, albeit yowling and struggling like a cat avoiding being dunked in a tub of water, to a new level of discipline in their work—planning and working to schedules, being held accountable. The biggest downside is that my nickname is Cruella De Vil. Well, we do share a love of dogs....

This experience has packed a lifetime of lessons into a very short time span. What I've learned to date will serve me well for the rest of my long and Scrappy life, and perhaps will be useful guides along your journey as well:

1. If you are held accountable but don't have authority, walk out.
2. If you don't walk out, find the person who does have authority and insist that they take responsibility. Don't view this as being powerless or as a compromise of your own personal authority. It's simply an organizational dysfunction beyond your control. But, with the right person at your side, it's not beyond your influence. (Also, find a good counselor. You may not think you can this time, but next time buckets of self-love will show you can walk out and survive!)
3. If the performance of any team member is not up to muster, raise the issue immediately to their attention. Raise it repeatedly and in the right forums and in a manner that you can prove irrefutably. Protecting nice but incapable people is no favor to anyone.

4. Never compromise your calculated analysis or gut feel. If you are measured by it, stick with your gut!

5. People scared to tell the truth in the first place will be terrified when they are forced to admit this later and will look for someone else to blame. Watch your back and have your backup plan ready!

6. Don't trust anyone else to deliver bad news. Do it yourself. You know what the real deal is and will speak with conviction. Senior people seem to have an aversion to proper "truth-speaking."

7. Corporate due prudence and wise business speak is often considered dishonest by people on the receiving end. No, it's not acceptable behavior. Avoid it like the plague!

8. Never for one nanosecond compromise any sensible business or project management principles. If you do, you will lose your self-worth, you will forever be seen as a "cretinous git" or a puppet or both, and you will lose all credibility.

9. If you land in a horrible business or project situation, the only way to recover is to apologize unreservedly. If the client is gracious enough to permit it, state your firm beliefs, and then show the details of your plan to make it right. Finally, make a clear commitment based on under-promising and over-delivering, remaining transparent in the extreme at every turn.

10. If a team has never had exposure to any good business or project management practices or methodologies, first pray, then tell them without a doubt what you expect of them and what they can expect from you. Once you have set these expectations, show the team how commitment works by putting yourself first in the firing line—always.

11. If you expect your team to work ungawdly hours, work with them, know what they are doing, ask questions, get involved, and become as tired as they are. Nothing else (other than pizza and sweet stuff) will endear you quicker than suffering with them when suffering is called for.

12. Everyone must be driven and measured by the same financial outcomes for true cooperation to exist.

13. **Know and believe in your own self-worth.** If you know this, you can't be flattered into an invidious position or fall for the ego-stroking approval trap from which you cannot easily extricate yourself. There are some challenges in life to which one can simply say, "No, thank you!"

14. **Don't forget to laugh!**

P.S. If you see some marbles rolling past your desk, those would be mine. Please collect them for me and post them back at your earliest convenience!

Terrie Mui

Catalyst in Making Visions Possible

Scrappy Kimberly says: *A truly Scrappy woman should be able to be able to parachute into a strange city, make a tent out of the parachute, and create an entirely new career and life for herself by sundown. That's exactly the image I have of Terrie Mui! In fact, she'd probably be sketching out a diagram of the major highways and features of the area on the way down in order to better navigate once she hit the ground. Say aloha to any preconceived notions of laid-back Hawaiians!*

My name is Terrie Mui, and I am a creative leader in launching new product development initiatives and developing workable strategies. Experienced in the aerospace, Internet and bio-tech industries, I have developed technically challenging hardware and software products by creating an environment for team success.

A certified PMP and Stanford APM, I have held positions such as Senior Program Manager and Project Guru in both startups and mature organizations, creating collaborative relationships to realize the company's visions. I earned a Master's Degree in Systems Engineering from the University of Southern California and a Bachelor's Degree in Mechanical Engineering from Loyola Marymount University, as well as hard knocks education in RF/Microwave Engineering.

I am a principal of Project-Catalysts Consulting, which provides coaching and training in product development, business process improvement, and customer relationship management. My no-nonsense approach has been useful in multiple high-tech industries and in sales, marketing, engineering, and operations organizations. Besides serving on the board of directors of nonprofit organizations, I am also an advocate of women in project management and founder of Women in Project Management. This Silicon Valley community, founded in 2002 and dedicated to women interested in the project management profession, mentors women to find their passion in project management or offer other ideas.

An accomplished cook and foodie, I relish bringing together different ingredients from around the world and sharing the creative output with my adventurous foodie friends.

"Well-behaved women seldom make history."
- *Laurel Thatcher Ulrich*

Chapter

7 Riding the Wave

Terrie Mui

Did you know that if you grow up in Switzerland you have to choose your profession while you're in high school? Only about 20 percent of the population continues on to the university level, and the remainder attends vocational school. If you want to change later, it's almost impossible—not because you don't have the potential or desire, but because change is slow in a country that has been around for a long, long, long time.

I would die in an environment like that! With the ever-changing economic environment, I've reinvented and refocused myself more than a few times, starting with my first year in college, and continuing the routine right up to the present. Yes, incredibly, I'm going through a transition yet again—right now—from a seasoned manager of multi-million dollar high-tech programs to a leadership educator and catalyst (and that's just one possibility I'm considering). How did a mechanical engineer with a master's degree in systems engineering end up as a program manager working in Silicon Valley, a software geek's heaven? Let's start from the beginning . . . in the warm, balmy breezes of beautiful Hawaii. Can't you just hear the ukuleles strumming in the distance?

Memories of a Displaced Hawaiian

My family delighted in telling stories of the blossoming of my organizational and leadership abilities in my childhood. I would tell my grandparents where to sit at the table when we had dinner. (Fortunately, they thought it was cute.) My ability to read maps was honed by guiding my mother through streets outside of Honolulu, although I could barely see over the dashboard at the time! My grandmother frequently reminded me "You are so bossy!" so it seems that I had the ability to lead early in life.

And if anyone happened to venture into my bedroom, they would have noticed something unusual for a child my age: clothes hung up and everything in its place. Not obsessively, but easily accessible. Clutter makes me nuts! So there is evidence that the organization gene was also in place way back then.

As far back as I remember, my family expected me to finish college and get a good job as a doctor, lawyer, or some other respectable professional. Being an independent person, I rejected these ideas outright. Who were they kidding?! I was this bossy kid, and wanted to define my future, knowing that it would somehow involve math and science. Those classes were interesting and I did well in them, although I thought art, music and philosophy were fun, too. When it came to toys, I favored the Air France model airplane my father gave me and the toy robot from Japan. Sure, dolls were cute, but they really didn't *do* anything except look pretty on the shelf. I had more fun building Barbie's dollhouse than drinking pretend tea. I would rather play with my racecar set in the living room!

When I started at the University of Hawaii, my classes were a collection something like this: advanced calculus, accounting, medical technology, art, psychology, chemistry, programming, world history, etc. It took a couple of semesters to decide to focus on computer science. Handheld calculators were just becoming prevalent, mercifully pushing slide rules into oblivion, and the power of computing seemed to me to have infinite possibilities! Now that my career was decided, it was time to leave Hawaii.

Everyone asks how I could leave such a beautiful place. It was wonderful when I was growing up, but it was time to leave "the nest" and explore the rest of the world.

City of Angels—Incoming!

After moving to Los Angeles to continue my studies, my first semester was a real eye-opener. Where were the Chinese restaurants? I can't wear my shorts and flip-flops—it's so cold! (It was like 68 degrees F.) Where are the blue skies and white clouds? What's that grey stuff in the sky? People kept asking me if I was Hawaiian. (No, I'm Chinese.) It was bit of a shock to look around and not see an ocean of black hair like mine. Instead of being of the majority, I was now in the minority (Asian from Hawaii) as well as a being a woman engineer. Oh well, that's the reality. Did it matter? Not at all!

After my first semester of computer science and electrical engineering courses, I noticed something about my coursework. Bottom line, the subjects were hard! Not that I didn't try, but I just did not get it. On the other hand, I relished my advanced courses in physics. The more "mechanical" concepts they involved were easier to visualize and far more interesting. The light bulb went off: change my major from computer science to mechanical engineering and take one more course for a minor in computer science. (Didn't want to waste those hard-earned credits!) I was the only female out of six mechanical engineering majors. Not a problem. There was no reason in my mind why I wouldn't be as good as the other students—and I was.

In what was supposed to be my final semester, I had a tough decision to make. Should I take a grueling load of 19 credits, including two graduate courses, or take fewer courses and attend for one more semester? Either way, I had to ask myself whether I was nuts. It made no sense to me to delay finishing my degree and pay for another semester just to take 5 credits. As I was both frugal and impatient at the time, I opted for the punishing workload and a quicker finish. And in spite of that, I did just fine—enjoying the last throes of college life by working like a dog.

Actually, I don't really remember much from those last four months except for a sense of studying some really cool stuff and a tremendous relief at my last final. And I think I had some beer now and then. Then I had to get a job, of course. Made me wonder why I'd been in such a hurry to graduate!

Next Step to Full Independence—Get a Job!

What kind of job? I had a mechanical engineering degree and had done a couple of summers at aerospace companies who wanted me to join them. But, to be quite honest, I didn't want to contribute to a product that might be used to hurt people. So, I worked my way into the transportation industry instead—diesel trucks to be exact. That lasted for less than two years because of the gas crisis that hit in the early 1980s. Fortunately, I did have a great manager who had no issues with a woman engineer (and who would?) and was a strong believer in training.

Moral qualms aside, I was fortunate to get a job in aerospace again because of a transferable skill, but in communications equipment for commercial satellites. How cool is that! I figured there wasn't much chance of people being communicated to death, although I've sat in some meetings that could prove that wrong.

Getting MAD—Mechanical Analysis or Design, That Is

Maybe you are familiar with what a mechanical engineer does for products, but if not I can sum it up in two words: design and analysis. Here's what I learned in the first year of this job: design is not my forte, nor am I passionate about doing finite element analysis, a fancy term for a rather complicated way of analyzing mechanical structures. I'm more interested in how the pieces go together, the big picture. Lucky for me, my manager's manager believed in developing people based on their passion and strengths. If it weren't for him, I wouldn't have been given the opportunity to become a project engineer, whatever that was. I surely didn't know at the time. But the job sounded interesting and challenging, so I took the leap.

Again, I lucked out and went to work for a really good project manager. He was more of a coach than a manager, which suited me just fine, and he provided plenty of valuable guidance and advice. In return, I kept him informed of critical issues and any questions that bubbled up around working with other project team members.

Transitioning a design to be manufactured consistently so it can fly around in space someday requires the expertise of many technical specialties—material scientists, electrical engineers, test engineers, and so on. Wouldn't you think there would be a difference of opinions when there was a problem? There were some, but the goals of the product were clear and everyone worked toward that goal. It was wonderful! Little did I know this kind of work environment was so rare. Life was just one long and relatively happy string of task lists and completed milestones.

Then I set a goal: I wanted to be a project manager before my thirtieth birthday. I don't know what it is about ages like thirty, forty, fifty and the like that inspires people to set such goals, but it worked for me. I made it by my twenty-ninth birthday. But, nothing's so sure to change as the economy, and my job shifted yet again. I became a manufacturing engineering manager, then a so-called program engineer (whatever that means), and finally the program manager of communications equipment for space satellites. Now that really was "out of this world" work. And I teamed with all the different groups in the company—from marketing to finance to manufacturing, managing budgets as well as the customer. I just loved the complexity and setting up the programs for success.

I've been in a senior project or program manager role ever since, in broadband communications, scientific instrumentation, and green-tech industries, not that my Scrappiness could ever be contained within my professional role. What I love about this work is that it's like running your own little company! The only difference is you don't cash in if you do a great job, and you don't go bankrupt if you really screw up.

Make Mine a Double

Was this hard, going through all of these changes? Well, I suppose so. As odd as it sounds, change is constant, and the current situation doesn't last forever. However, there is always a choice in how you view the situation: half full or half empty. Only you can choose how to view your life. I choose half full. (And if it's a nice glass of chardonnay or pinot, even better!)

Not that it was all wine and roses during these periods. Of course there were periods of depression, self-doubt, and uncertainty! That's called "being human." These were also opportunities for personal evaluation and growth, a time to check if I was living the life I wanted to live. It's simple, but not easy.

There were twelve to fourteen hour days, seven days a week, for months at a time, because of the almighty schedule. Being the last one in the office was also a common occurrence. And there were also times of incredibly fast learning curves, being the new person asking the basic questions. Was that hard? Only on the ego. But walking the path of the novice in a new job was a necessary part of quickly developing the working knowledge of the product and the company. It also developed my support network within the company. People love to share their knowledge with someone who's sincerely interested. I established some terrific relationships with people during those times, and really understand the phrase, "Hit the ground running!"

"No Pressure, but the Company's Future Depends on You"

The programs I've managed always had some type of strategic significance to the company, therefore some bit of pressure to succeed (imagine that!). In one program, there was a performance issue that multiple teams were working to resolve by focusing on their portion of the product. But that was a little like trying to fix a flat tire by cutting it up into parts and having different groups work on each piece. This program impacted a significant percentage of our deliveries (that means revenue, baby!), and the current approach wasn't getting the job done. Drastic action was needed!

Forming a small "tiger team," we took a broad view of the entire issue, called "systems thinking," and created experiments to explore the possible causes. We had the best minds on this team, both theoretical and practical, and we found the problem after only three attempts. And did we have a good laugh when we found it! It was so simple—the darn thing just wasn't being built straight. (Oh, what's a few millimeters among friends?)

Was it risky to start this team? Yeah, you bet, since it was considered a bit rebellious to start yet *another* team to work on this problem when so many others were already tackling it from their own perspective. (Can you imagine how the other teams felt?) And the effort might not have provided a solution.

Working under such pressure and high visibility was stressful, so we used humor to keep the problem in perspective. This really helped us to be more creative as well as objective. Yes, there are Ph.D.s who have a sense of humor. Wild and outrageous scenarios were suggested, and we laughed our asses off at the crazy ones, but eventually there were a few that didn't seem so crazy. Those are the ones we tried, and it worked. I learned a wonderful lesson from this experience: include laughter in your work. There is a camaraderie that forms when a group can laugh together—work doesn't seem like work anymore.

Then there was the most challenging program of all. The team was so frustrated with the lack of success during the product development phase that they started pointing fingers at each other, blaming each other as the cause of the many delays. It was ugly. My interview consisted of listening to all the interviewers identify the issues in the program, then asking me, "So, are you still interested in the position?" OMG! Sure, why not? Sounds like a challenge. Yeah, right! What was I thinking?!

When I first started this job, I attempted to work within the existing team structure, but I couldn't create the team management environment needed to be successful. My next tactic was to restructure the team roles and set a clear direction. Politically, this was very risky because of the emotional impact to people that I was going to displace and the closeness between some of the team members. I discussed my devious plans with my manager and he backed me 100 percent when we moved ahead. There were lots and lots and lots of meetings with these team members in which we made every attempt to be respectful of their inputs. Still, there were some hurt feelings. Time does heal all wounds. After a few years, I think the hard feelings faded, but it's still tough on the relationships when you kick people off of a team.

As we moved beyond that little rough patch of road, we managed to take time to laugh. Sometimes it was playing with squeeze toys in our team meetings (for stress relief!) or bouncing red balls down the hallway. (Really, Mr. President, the ball just ran down the hallway for no reason whatsoever!) Laughter provided some relief for the pressure, and it often inspired creative ideas to address the difficult issues.

The challenges presented by these two programs helped me clearly define what it takes to get a team moving towards a goal and how people are alike but also oh so different. I also had the opportunity to identify my strengths and where I needed help. Each project, initiative, and program that I managed resulted in a powerful set of "lessons learned" that I used later in a variety of companies at different stages of maturity.

My Crystal Ball Is Becoming Clear!

At some point in my career, I noticed that I was easily able to predict at the outset what would drive the success of a particular program and what would be the major risks. I guess I eventually started to recognize the same problems and challenges I'd seen before. Time seemed to slow, and I started to anticipate change and define alternative plans instead of reacting to every little problem. I learned to stand back and observe the situation instead of being emotionally involved or tied to a particular solution. Not that there weren't other surprises that seemed to fall out of the sky, but my confidence in deciding how to handle a situation had increased dramatically.

There was a time I never would have thought that I could be on a board of directors, let alone the president, of a nonprofit organization. But one day the opportunity presented itself. It took a giant leap in believing in me, trusting that I could learn to do what was needed to be successful in this role. My learning curve was shortened by asking others about their challenges and reading about real-world business strategy examples. I found that I could apply my skills and knowledge from my for-profit experience to the nonprofit world.

But I did need to understand the priorities of a nonprofit, the main difference being more focus on the service being provided rather than the profit that they made. (I guess that's why they call them "nonprofits"!) There was always a financial aspect to consider—what can we afford? There was only enough money to pay for the most essential people, and having a great team of volunteers was a keystone to success. Managing volunteers is much different than managing employees, let me tell you! It's like bodybuilding your influence muscles!

Dot-com and/or Bust!

In the dot-bust period of 2001, I became part of the RIF (reduction in force) population. I was crushed! I had trusted my manager to keep me aware of the business environment and to take care of me. And weren't jobs supposed to last forever? Welcome to the brave new world of the 21st century!

After about a month of thrashing around with all this free time, and seeing quite a few of my colleagues in the same situation, I got this idea that we could help each other with our job search and career issues. Thus began the Women in Project Management (WiPM) group, now known as the Women's Forum. We had this great idea for a logo, but decency and good taste demanded that we abandon it....

This kind of group is now called a "success team," so we were a bit ahead of our time. Forming this group was not difficult, since I had a very clear purpose in mind and knew who would be involved. I recruited several other like-minded women, and we started the organization by developing the mission statement that we still use today:

"The WiPM Forum's mission is to provide a community for women interested in the project management profession, focused on mutual growth and sharing of knowledge through informal meetings, networking, and mentoring. Through mutual sharing the group seeks to provide insights into project management issues common to multiple industries. This interaction enables participants to make significant positive changes to their work environment."

We were able to successfully support every single person to find a new position in those early days. Since then the group has grown to over two hundred people and meets monthly as part of the local PMI chapter activities.

Same Old Way? No Way!

Now, everything I've accomplished may have been accomplished by following all the rules, but I knew there was a better way. Frequently, in order to get anything done in a timely manner, I found it was worthwhile to study the current process, figure out what could be done to improve it, and then convince people to use my ideas instead of falling into the temptation of doing things the same old way. Whether it was a multi-million dollar proposal approval or a straightforward risk mitigation plan, my approach was to ask everyone involved in the process for *their* ideas to make their job easier. Pulling these ideas together, aligning them with the current company goals, and defining the new way of doing things made it possible to get the support of the appropriate management types.

But I'm not always that diplomatic...or patient! There were other times that I simply implemented the change without asking for "permission." That was much faster, but not without a certain level of consequences. Starting the first Statistical Process Control (SPC) initiative (closely related to "Six Sigma" methods) in my division of Boeing by creating cross-functional teams that addressed product and process issues was one of those occasions. I really didn't have the support of the manufacturing manager when the first team was started. But I knew that the idea was sound, had been successful in other companies, and would reduce costs by improving the product. Looking back now, I can clearly see that having his support would have helped with the management alignment that is considered so critical these days. But, hey, I just did it. And, fortunately for me, it worked.

Over the course of my career, the decision to take action was usually based on what I thought was the right thing to do for the people involved in the context of the business environment at the time. "What is needed to make these people's jobs easier, faster, and more interesting?" I'd ask myself. I believed having that focus would help to get them on board. And I knew that they would know more than I would about the changes needed and, if I could just get them to share their ideas with me, I knew I could help them. It's a win-win for everyone! Sometimes the ideas were, shall we say, very creative (a nice way of saying "wild and crazy"), but most of the time they made sense. I've found that people often have ideas about how to do their jobs better, but they seem to be waiting for someone to invite them to take action. I'm always happy to extend that invitation and support them.

Someone Must Have Said This to Me Sometime...

Uncovering the layers of my life experience by writing this chapter has helped me distill some insights that may be helpful to you. I know I have heard this wisdom from numerous sources, but I have not really understood the significance of these principles until recently.

1. "If you don't know where you're going, any path will get you there." **Set a goal** and go for it! It doesn't have to be a lifelong goal; it can be something on the horizon in the next three months. Having a goal comes from knowing what you want, which is partially based on the next principle.

2. **Know what you value.** Honesty, integrity, relationships, money? I have fifteen values that I've used to guide me over the course of my life, and a "top five" that I'm currently using. These top five change over time, but the list of fifteen stays constant. Do you know your top fifteen values? It's worth taking time to mull this over and make your values list.

3. **Know who you are.** Patient, quiet, boisterous, introverted, analytical? There are numerous psychological assessments available that can provide insights. Many are free. Good friends can also be a helpful mirror for you if you ask. Just be sure you're ready to hear their opinions before you ask! Then ask yourself if this is who you want to be. If not, define a plan to change and become the kind of person you *do* want to be.

4. It's your life and, therefore, **it's always your choice.** Be responsible for your decisions. Don't give away your power. Know that you *always* have a choice of what you do, how you feel, and how you behave.

5. Lastly, **what's your mission?** An insightful comment from Keith Ferazzi's book *Never Eat Alone* was that people basically have one of three missions: making money, changing the world, or finding love. My mission is changing the world. Knowing my mission helps me align my goals with my values, and my daily activities to what I consider "success" and personal satisfaction.

What more could you want?

Part III

How to Succeed in Business by Really, *Really* Trying

After leaving HP, I went on a roller coaster ride through a succession of Silicon Valley startups that left me feeling alternately giddy and sick to my stomach. They all ultimately failed. Not that this bothered me much—you're no one in Silicon Valley if you haven't ridden at least one company completely into the ground. When I first left HP, I did so while passing up a sizable severance package. (I could have laid myself off six months later and potentially gotten a year's salary for my trouble.) But I was more than ready to leave, and money just wasn't enough to keep me there. I let go five of my team of seven guys as compassionately as I could, laid myself off, and joined Candescent, now a $700 million crater just south of San Jose.

Working at a startup made me feel as if my work was making a positive difference, an illusion I'd lost in the big company environment of HP. It was so exciting to feel that what I did every day could impact the bottom line results, and I threw myself into my work with my usual fierce resolve to achieve what was considered unlikely or impossible. But it turned out that we really *were* doing the impossible, and within six months I was among the sixty chosen ones in the first wave of layoffs. This was no surprise to me—I could see it coming, and had already started storing most of my office stuff in my car trunk in the preceding weeks. The VP who delivered the news tried to comfort me, but I was in no mood for his sympathy and just said, "Hey, I was looking for work when I found this job." Besides, I was happy to be out of there! Although I had hoped to find a fast-paced work environment where results mattered more than politics (I can dream, can't I?), Candescent seemed to have all the problems of a big company with none of the advantages of a small one. I failed forward to my next tumultuous adventure, ReplayTV.

When I started working at ReplayTV during the dot-com boom, it seemed as close to a sure thing as any company in the "Silicon Valley lottery" could be. I mean, who wouldn't want to pause live television and skip commercials?! Plus the team was incredibly talented, and we willingly worked like dogs to accomplish miracles month after month. Cracks began to appear in our business model, however, and before long the writing was on the wall. The day after we delivered the product to the warehouse, I realized that I had pushed myself and others beyond reasonable limits for nothing more than another set-top box. Did I really need to drive myself to exhaustion and become a person I couldn't stand (let's not use the "B" word, let's just say "super grouchy") in order to bring this product to market? I'll always value the enormous amount I learned there, and cherish the precious relationships that have far outlasted the company, but the "Showstopper" was a product ahead of its time. (With a name like "Showstopper" I should have known this project was cursed from the start!) I lingered awhile under the protection of one of the few executives I hadn't alienated with my "call a spade a friggin' shovel" style, but I was obviously going nowhere at this company after burning so many bridges in the name of getting this impossible project done. Clearly I had once again fallen into a familiar trap—creating a success that I could not benefit from due to the relationships I'd damaged along the way. It was time to fail forward once again. I left shortly before the long slide to bankruptcy began.

Every "failure" in my career so far had resulted in a promotion and a raise, and this was no exception. It was the year 2000, and I joined a spinoff from Xerox PARC, an organization famous for their inability to commercialize their own inventions. The company was called Groupfire, which foreshadowed that we'd all be fired as a group when the venture capitalists took back all of their money during the imminent dot-com bust. It was my first executive position, and the salary was about twice what I imagined I'd ever earn in my entire lifetime when I was a child. (The salary offered was $40,000 more per year than I was going to ask for. Good thing I read that book on negotiations! Unless you're skilled at "anchoring," the person who mentions money first loses. Hold out for the offer, ladies!) I was the VP of Program Management, and I added "Organizational Effectiveness" to my responsibilities as well, because I wanted to do a great cultural experiment. I felt I was finally in a position to shape the culture of a company to the ideal that I'd been seeking since my HP days, and I was eager to implement everything I'd learned about leadership and company culture in this thirty-person startup. And experiment I did, holding organization-wide discussions of company values, organizing monthly decompression recreational activities, and abolishing performance appraisals in favor of more frequent and effective ways of aligning individual performance with company objectives.

In past jobs I had been more focused on results than relationships, which made me rather useful when some impossible project needed to be completed, but somewhat unpopular with the people I rode roughshod over to get the job done. When I joined Groupfire, I promised myself that I wouldn't be a hit man for hire anymore—someone brought in to do the dirty jobs, but never invited to dinner with the beautiful people. I was also determined to benefit from the success I helped create, rather than alienating myself through the methods used to create that success. To achieve this I'd have to balance the importance of both results and relationships. And, when push came to shove, I'd have to make relationships just a tad more important than results.

As I am genetically predisposed to be an unstoppable force of nature obsessed with results, it took every ounce of willpower to keep my promise to myself, but it turned out to be a good choice. Within seven short months the company went entirely out of business, and we all went our separate ways. Because of my choice to prioritize relationships over results, I ended my time at Groupfire with much healthier relationships with my colleagues than I ever had in the past. And to my surprise I didn't have to sacrifice results—I just had to be a bit more patient, a trifle more tactful, and pay a whole lot more attention to the human side of business. This turned out to be great practice for my next job—running my own consulting business.

When I started my business in 2001, it was the worst economy in recent memory. I had half-heartedly started a consulting business several years before, but quickly got sucked into the allure of a steady paycheck when my first client booked me solid and then hired me full-time. But by now I knew with absolute certainty that I was not born to be an employee. I simply don't have the constitution to sit idly by collecting my pay while the train jumps off the track, and I find it incredibly difficult to resist telling everyone else how things could be done better. It finally hit me. I was born to be a consultant! "Consultants are paid to be opinionated and mouthy," one of my ex-bosses told me. If so, I was a perfect match for that profession! I launched Wiefling Consulting and vowed never to take a "real" job again.

Since I was getting started in the throes of something akin to economic spastic colon, I knew it would take perseverance to grow a successful business ("The first five years are the hardest," I'd been told!), so I committed to myself that I'd keep going for at least three months after I wanted to give up. This promise turned out to be vital to my success, as the first three years were tougher than a cut of beef in economy seating. I hadn't worked so hard to make so little money since my grass-cutting days in high school! Although everyone said I had a lot of value to offer, I literally couldn't give it away. Sometimes I'd drive thirty miles to earn $60. I did everything I could think of to grow my business, but mostly I just hung on through the first two years while the economy tossed me around like a ball in a BINGO machine. But eventually I caught a few lucky breaks, and my revenue tripled, then doubled again, then doubled again, and I found myself making more money in a month than I'd made in a year during the early days.

The consulting life agreed with me. I felt more in control of my destiny, and I was highly motivated to be nicer to everyone because, well, you never know who might be your next client. (Heck, if I'd have known the relationships would last longer than the jobs—and some companies—I would have been nicer to people throughout my career!) And I didn't mind people wasting my time as much (a hot button of mine) when they were paying me by the hour.

Eventually I fell into an incredibly lucky opportunity, the sort that only the well-prepared experience. I did a bit of work for a Japanese company, which eventually led to my collaboration with ALC Education, Inc., headquartered in Tokyo, Japan. I met the incredible

Yuko Shibata, one of the authors in this book. Over the past five years, we've created a global management consultancy that helps international Japanese companies expand globally. What many people don't realize is that Japan, with only 130 million people, is the #2 economy in the world. With one-tenth the population of China, its economy was still the same size as China's as of 2009. And Japan's impact on the economic health of the world, while also frequently underappreciated, is enormous.[9] ALC, Yuko, and I, along with a band of consultants from the Silicon Valley, are on a mission to transform the Japanese economy for the good of the world. We're accomplishing this ridiculous goal one individual at a time, by shifting the mindset of leaders in Japanese companies, using techniques experts assured me would never work in the Japanese business culture. (Yet another example of why you should never accept expert opinions as the final word on what's possible. For more examples, see pretty much any article in a reputable source over the past couple of centuries where some famous, well-respected expert says something is impossible. In my experience, when you hear an expert claiming something's unrealistic, not feasible, or impossible, you can be fairly sure it's going to happen in the next decade or so.) We've worn a path in the sky travelling to Japan dozens of times over the past five years, and the results have been nothing short of startling.

Imagine an energetic blond woman from the U.S. being wildly successful in Japanese business! It's something I myself would have said was impossible a decade ago, but it happened nonetheless. Now most of my consulting work is for Japanese companies, mainly in Japan, but also in Europe and the U.S. One of my friends claims that this arrangement works well because I'm nothing like a Japanese woman, so I'm more or less a gender-neutral alien to my Japanese colleagues, which might explain why I've experienced basically zero gender bias in my work there. Another theorizes that the relationship works because neither party totally understands what the other is saying. Whatever the reason, I know from personal experience that widespread stereotypes of traditional, conservative Japanese businessmen (yes, they're still mostly men) are outdated. If I've learned anything at all about my Japanese colleagues, it's that they will do anything required for the greater good of the community, which the

---

9. "Japan's Technology Champions: Invisible but Indispensable," *The Economist*, November 5, 2009.

most global-minded among them take to be the population of the world. It's been said that failure's not fatal, but it is in Japan, and we push these guys to extremely uncomfortable limits in pursuit of their leadership development. (When I'm asking them to take big risks I sometimes joke that I want them to push the limits so far that, should they fail, they would bring shame on themselves and their families for generations to come. It's kind of an exaggeration...) I've come to greatly admire the people I've worked with, and I'm honored to be working with the ALC team to transform the planet through these Japanese companies and their commitment to solving global problems profitably.

As a consultant there are good years and there are bad years, but all in all, I prefer a bad year in consulting to a good year as an employee any day. At least I have only myself to blame for any negative business results. And I no longer have to trade my dignity and self-esteem for a paycheck, something I felt I regularly did as an employee. Now I choose my work, my partners, and my clients in alignment with my professional and personal values. Most employees aren't so lucky. I truly enjoy my work, something less than 20 percent of employees say, according to the Gallup Institute.[10] Most importantly, I feel free to be me. Ah, breathe into that!

I think every woman owes it to herself to explore the possibility of starting, running, and growing her own business. Sure, it's fraught with risk, setbacks and learning things the hard way. But it's been among the most gratifying experiences of my life, and I wouldn't have missed this adventure for anything in the world. A mere fifteen years ago, I didn't dare think that I could start my own business. Then I started hanging out with people like the sort who wrote the chapters in this section—Betty Jo, Julie, Nathalie, and Sue. Women much like these Scrappy entrepreneurs opened my eyes to the possibility that I could indeed have my own business. It turns out that all I had to do was make up a title, print up some business cards, start handing them out, and, as Julie advises, begin telling people I was in business. And just like Julie experienced, they believed me! Yup, when I believed, they believed. Imagine that!

---

10. Tom Rath and Jim Harter, *Well-Being: The Five Essential Elements* (New York: Gallup Press, 2010).

Blaze your own trail, but learn from the stories of these Scrappy Businesswomen first!

- Scrappy Kimberly

"The mind is not a vessel to be filled, but a fire to be kindled."
- *Plutarch*

Betty Jo Waxman

Scrappy Independent Consultant, Personal & Professional Development Trainer, and Lively Workshop Facilitator

Scrappy Kimberly says: *Why do I consider this woman Scrappy? ENERGY! If you're going to achieve seemingly impossible results, you can't drag yourself slug-like through the day, slumping in your chair and propping your eyelids open with toothpicks. Lethargic people don't get much done, and are unlikely to inspire Scrappy people to do anything besides flee from their presence. Betty Jo Waxman could power a small village simply by hooking electrodes to her earlobes.*

I work around the globe as an independent consultant delivering experiential workshops in the areas of leadership, communication, business, relationships, and self-awareness. My primary business is as a Senior Trainer for Productive Learning & Leisure, where I've been building this company alongside the founders for twenty-six years. My style of interacting with people makes it safe for them to discover and learn. I'm passionate about my work and dedicated to providing high value and making a positive difference in the lives of the participants in my programs. I live in San Rafael, California, with my husband Richard and our two children, Jordan and Rebecca. My hobbies include CrossFit training and "adventure travel." My burning desire is to live life with no regrets—I'm going to look back and shout, "Wahooo!"

"You must do the thing you think you cannot do."
- *Eleanor Roosevelt,* American Humanitarian and First Lady

Chapter

8 | Mindset, Baby, Mindset!

Betty Jo Waxman

Want to start your own business? You could read one (or many) of the hundreds of books out there on the subject, make all the right moves, and do it just the way the experts tell you to. Knock yourself out in the process! Will it get you all the way to the finish line? Possibly, but if you're missing one particular key ingredient of success, more than likely you will wind up someplace short of your dream destination. I can assure you that all the information in the world—and all the blood, sweat, and tears to go with it—won't get you to your personal nirvana if your mindset is out of whack. What am I suggesting? A gut check! But wait a minute. I just said *mind*set, and now I'm telling you to do a *gut* check? Stay with me and answer these questions truthfully.

Gut Check Time: No Fooling Yourself with This Much at Stake

> ## Gut Check Questions for the Aspiring Business Owner
>
> 1. Are you ready, willing, and able to work ridiculously long hours?
> 2. Will you vow to make time a "non-issue?" That means no complaining that there's "not enough time for me" (what you do for your business *is* for you). No using "I don't have enough time" as an excuse. For anything!
> 3. Are you up for hard work, doing jobs you don't want to do, and getting little, if any, pay for it? (At least at the onset.)
> 4. Are you good at selling, or at least *willing* to sell and get good at it?
> 5. Are you able to take on all of this and, at the same time, maintain a predominantly upbeat, determined attitude?

If you hear anything but a deafening "YES" rattling between your ears, or if your stomach tightens up because you really *want* it to be a "yes" but it just isn't (that's the gut check part), you have some work to do if you want to start, run, and grow your own business.

I once led a breakout session for a "Women in Business" conference with the topic, "So You Think You Want to Be an Entrepreneur?" Attendance was high. It just sounds like a dream come true to own your own business. Flexible hours. No boss to answer to. You take home all the profits. What could be better? Everyone wanted to get the inside track, so it was standing room only. Ten minutes into the presentation, the excitement had drained out of the room and I was about the least favorite person they could imagine. Why? Because I started out with the "gut check" questions above. You see, far too many women look at the proposition of owning a business and initially only see the upside. "How great to work for myself!" they muse. "What could be better than being my own boss? I can take off whenever I want to, and all the money will go to me!" Well, yes, but....

Start, run, and grow a business in the real world. While appealing, it's not for the faint of heart. It takes work and a willingness to make mistakes, feel stupid, look stupid, and then get right back up, make adjustments, and go after it again. It takes courage. It takes determination. And you'd better be able to sell. And perhaps the most challenging aspect is that you have to come to terms with the fact that you don't know it all. You'd better be very willing to *quickly* ask for the help you will unavoidably need. Might as well tackle that one right off the bat.

"Lone Rangers" Need Not Apply

It's your business, but you don't have to do it all yourself. I facilitate a workshop titled "The Mind in Business" that is designed to help illuminate the blind spots people have when looking at their own business. The assignment they are given at the end of session one involves coming up with an idea, and then executing on it when they return to class the following week. I give them the guidelines and offer an array of examples of what has been done in the past. I end with an invitation to contact me directly for assistance with the process. I direct them to a stack of my business cards, and repeat the offer of assistance—twice.

I've done this somewhere around forty times. The group size is anywhere from fifteen to thirty participants. Never have more than two people from any given group reached out for assistance. Usually no one contacts me! What's more shocking is that when we return in week two, we discuss how they went about doing the assignment, what went through their minds, and what (if any) actions they took. Scarcely any of them even *remember* that I offered assistance. Those who heard me report dismissing my sincerity, or admit remembering that I said something about helping them, but say that *it never occurred to them to ask for help*. This is problematic! If you are in business for yourself and trying to reinvent the wheel, or think that you can do it all yourself, you are making it much harder than it needs to be. If, like me, you believe that what we selectively hear and don't hear is no accident, read on.

There are several possible reasons for going it alone. If that's your inclination, I strongly suggest gaining some understanding as to what that is all about. Maybe it's your ego—not your gut—that needs to be checked. If your identity is wrapped up in being able to say "I did it *all* myself," that need is going to hamper your effectiveness in the business world. If you're convinced that nobody can do it as well as you can, a.k.a. "if you want something done right, you have to do it yourself," then the limitations are fairly obvious: you are confined to what is attainable within your personal capacity, and the "growing" part of your business is going to get dicey very quickly. There are reasons for these personal beliefs, but suffice it to say that they are not universal truths, and, therefore, it's incumbent upon you to address them, sooner rather than later, if you really want to succeed.

Know Yourself: Better Now Than Later, After You've Gone Too Far...

Too far down the wrong road, that is. I can make a case for this in just about every area of life, but when it comes to starting your own business, the first application of the age-old principle "know thyself" is what *type* of business owner you will be. There are at least four different models of business ownership. Starting a business without considering the pros and cons of each as they relate to who you are, what you are good at, and most importantly, what you just flat out *aren't* going to do, is unnecessarily risky.

Models of Business Ownership|
(OK, it's simplified, but plenty for starters.)

1. **Own a company.** This comes complete with staff, payroll, departments, org charts, and all of the systems that come with operating an organization.

2. **Be self-employed.** Develop a product or service that you market, sell, and deliver basically by yourself. Whatever it takes to get your product or service out the door is on your shoulders.

3. **Own a franchise.** Buy a franchise and build it according to the formula and within the guidelines established by the parent company. They've done the heavy lifting on structure and development, you execute on the predetermined strategy.

4. **Be an independent contractor.** Work on an ongoing series of projects for a variety of businesses that contract for your services. Market yourself, sell yourself, and then deliver.

If you fail to select the model that fits your preferences, you could be headed for early disappointment. One example of this shows up frequently in the experiential workshop I mentioned earlier, "The Mind in Business," which is made up of people who own their business or make their money through sales. Many participants are shocked to discover that they have created a business that falls into category #2—they work for themselves—yet they went off on their own anticipating the benefits that come with #1. They find themselves with no time off, struggling with aspects of the business that they have no skill for or interest in, and having relatively little time to do what they went off on their own to do in the first place—deliver the product or service they love. When asked what they were thinking before starting a business, they generally say things like, "Well, I was doing what I love, but got tired of someone else making money off of my work, so I figured I'd go out on my own, work less, and make more." How romantic! How idealistic! There's no faster way to appreciate all that it takes to run a business than to hang out your shingle and post the "open for business" sign.

Before you hang out that shingle, do your research and be brutally honest with yourself about why you are making such a move. This moment of introspection will be a big help when choosing which model you are going to pursue. If you are never going to put in the time to attain the right attitude, and to learn how to sell, then I'd strongly suggest choosing a model in which you don't need to do that. Get a partner. Hire a sales staff. Nothing sells itself.

It's important to know that every one of the four models above has huge upsides, depending on who you are. I know people who are extremely successful in each of these (and, by the way, I also know people who have just as much success in "employee" positions). I also know people who have failed miserably in each model. There is no formula for this, there are no guarantees, and there are no shortcuts when it comes to knowing yourself.

No "Either/Or" Thinking Permitted

You can start, run, and grow your own business without sacrificing your health or relationships. There's a lot of bad press out there about "balance." I think it is a very misunderstood concept, one that no one really thinks about too deeply; they just throw it out there when they get tired in some area of their life and don't know what else to chalk it up to. What is balance anyway? Devoting an equal amount of time to several areas of your life? What if all areas of your life don't *need* the same amount of time? I consider my physical well being a very important part of my life, and giving that area an hour a day, along with making good food choices, keeps me in pretty good shape. Am I out of balance because I spend so much more time in other areas?

I don't think balance has anything to do with time. I think it's more about not resisting what we are doing. We make choices that have us in relationships, or in business, and then we don't do the things necessary to keep those areas healthy. Make your choices and then come to peace with them. If they aren't working well, make new choices when it is appropriate to do so. I know countless individuals who work what most people would consider "a lot," and have a deep feeling of joy and balance. By the same token, I often meet people who insist that if they had more time they could create balance. When more time becomes available, they just fill it with more of exactly what they are already doing. This leads to the same end result, and they feel even more out of balance.

The best suggestion I can make here: when you go into business for yourself, do what you do with joy, and recognize that you brought it into your life. When you don't insist on making time a factor (or an excuse!), you'll find a way to nurture all that is truly important to you. If you don't come from a place of joy and choice, you're liable to succeed in business and then resent that you did, especially if you think it's what caused your health or relationships to suffer.

No "I Did It and So What?" Outcomes

Connect your business to something bigger. Sometimes you are going to get tired. You are going to look at yourself in the mirror and ask, "Why did I do this?" When that happens, you'd better have a really good answer! Whenever you experience an ounce of doubt, you need to be able to go straight to what I call your personal "What For?" Why *are* you doing this? You need to tie your work and your business to something that means an awful lot to you to get through these defining moments. Once you do, it stops being about you, and you will fuel yourself with a desire that will enable you to overcome those tough times. Without a deeper reason than having a business or making a living, you'll likely give up before you reach the finish line, or you'll be successful and wonder why you went through it all...because you'll feel surprisingly unsatisfied.

I have a relative who spent a lifetime in the medical field as a highly respected doctor. He told me on several occasions how it was never very satisfying for him. It was his parents' dream that he become a doctor, but it was never his dream. Don't live out someone else's dream! Do something in the world that resonates with *you* and do what matters most to *you*. It sounds simple, because it is, but it's still the most important piece of the puzzle. Get busy jigsawing!

Where Do You Think I Learned All This Stuff?

I actually passed up a chance to own my own business early in my career. My parents owned a chain of women's clothing stores that had been in the family for several generations. I knew a lot about business from growing up in it. I worked part-time in our stores beginning at the age of ten. I started out sorting hangers, opening boxes, hanging newly delivered merchandise, and making a tag for every item before it was taken out onto the selling floor. When I was old enough, I was given the responsibility of keeping track of what was being sold and what inventory needed to be transferred from one store to another. I stayed behind the scenes because I was too young to be trusted by the customers in giving them fashion advice.

Eventually, I was allowed to go behind the desk and write up sales. (This was before computer technology, and we painstakingly wrote out sales slips by hand.) I was a whiz during the holidays behind the gift-wrap counter, and to this day I can wrap a package perfectly at lightning-fast speed. Once I hit high school, I graduated to the sales floor and started to build my experience of taking care of people. That's what you do when you're really good at sales—take care of people. My mom was the best at this, and I listened to her interactions with customers from the time I was tall enough to see over the counter.

My parents worked together in the business. My mother did the buying, and when she had time she would work with customers to really understand what they wanted. My dad was the financial wizard, and was also excellent with personnel. I came back to work alongside them after finishing graduate school. For four years they groomed me to take over the business, as they were nearing retirement. When the time came, I couldn't take the reins. It was their dream, not mine.

After twenty-eight years of seeing the business world through the eyes of an owner, I went to work as an employee for an organization that offers personal and professional development seminars. From the very first day, I worked like I owned the place. I simply don't know any other way to go about my work! After ten years, I took a five-year hiatus to be with our young children. When it was time to return to work, I took option #4 above—I became an independent contractor. I wish I could say it was a conscious choice after a thoughtful process, the kind of process I just advised you to use when starting your own business. But it wasn't. It was convenient, something I could do part-time. And I eventually realized that it was (and still is) a perfect fit for me, who I am, what I'm willing to do, and—most importantly—what I'm *not* willing to do.

And here's how I rank on the gut check. I have no problem "working" a lot. I put that in quotation marks because many times I find myself in the middle of my work and can honestly say that there is *nothing* I'd rather be doing. It just doesn't feel like work! Putting in long hours doing things I sometimes don't get paid for, as I sometimes do, is a non-issue for me as well because I choose to see everything I do as a step, a lurch, or a leap towards where I'm headed. I don't get caught up in connecting my actions with my results to fit a direct cause-and-effect paradigm. I know I can't always draw a direct line from every activity to a precise end result or a specific amount of money in my bank account. But, thanks to the accumulation of actions, I keep moving forward, and this approach has worked extremely well for me. I can honestly say I have no idea how many hours I work. I have no interest in adding them up and dividing my income by the total, then dealing with how it will make me feel when I tell myself some story about whether I'm working "too much" for what I'm getting paid (or whatever other nonsense is connected to an arbitrary number). That probably best exemplifies the attitude I bring to my business.

As for selling, I am married to the quintessential salesman; he loves his craft, he is brilliant at it, and he has the healthiest sales mindset I have ever witnessed. Combine that with my history of watching my mother sell, and delight her customers in the process, and I end up with a pretty good foundation. Still, I have my moments. When selling myself to gain a contract, I do take that extra time to prepare and remind myself of my value. If I don't, my husband takes it upon himself to do that for me! Otherwise, I could sell myself short (pun intended). I work on sales constantly. If I didn't, I wouldn't be where I am today.

When it comes to asking for help, I'm sure I have my own blind spots. But growing up the youngest, and always having someone around who knew more than I did, it's not really a problem for me to solicit help. My husband might argue this one; I can sometimes bristle at unsolicited advice from him if I go unconscious, even though in retrospect his direction is usually pretty darned useful. Typically I will go to experts, or anyone I know who is more experienced and knowledgeable than I am, in order to solve a problem or make progress more quickly. I have never thought that asking for help was an indication of my lack of ability. I know what I know, and what I don't know, somebody else knows. Besides, most people love to help other people, and when I ask for it I usually get a "happy to help" reply. I must say that I, too, give my assistance pretty freely when someone bothers to ask. I give often, knowing that it's only a matter of time before I'll be on the other side of the helping equation.

The independent contractor role is a perfect fit for me, but I have to say that it's been a bit of good fortune that I discovered that. I started out going that route because it just worked for my situation, and I've grown to love every aspect of it. Personally, I wouldn't want to own a big company. Planning, budgeting, structuring, creating a vision, and leading a group of people are all nice, but not part of my dream. I'm in love with my work—with rolling up my sleeves, delivering the service, and being with people as they grow, evolve, and become more aware human beings. Working in this capacity allows me the freedom to do what I do best most of the time. Such a deal!

I am blessed to have business relationships that span almost thirty years with some of my closest friends. We work together in an organization that is my primary contract. My husband and I get peripherally involved in one another's businesses because our lives blend together through all of it. I grew up seeing my parents live and work together (unbelievable as it seems these days, they only had one car!), so it doesn't occur to me that success in one area causes anything but more success in the other. Though, again, my husband would make a case for me going, going, and going like the Energizer Bunny, and sometimes going straight to sleep right after dinner in order to recharge when I start to wear down. I'm OK with that. My doctor says I have the health of a woman fifteen years younger (not the body or the face, just the health!), so what I do is working pretty well for me.

Find Out What You're Here to Do, and DO IT!

My work is my passion. I believe with every bone in my body that my work is having a powerful, productive, positive impact on the world. Not just my world, *the* world. I have spent many years discovering what I am here to do and then doing it. I am filled with certainty that my actions and efforts are in alignment with my purpose for existing. This thoughtful reflection on a reason for being is a process that I encourage everyone to undertake. I don't do my work for the money, for the glamour, or for my ego. I do it because it is who I am, and it's making a meaningful difference. Even though money isn't my motivation, I do quite well financially, I have traveled the world as part of my work, and my self-esteem is as healthy as the rest of me.

There's a reason I told my story at the end of this chapter. We actually do come last when it comes to running our own business, at least in the short run. We do things even when we don't feel like it, because it matters to our customers and there's no one else to do them. We give up time for ourselves, because the quality of what needs to get out the door is more important that a little more leisure time. For me, that's part of the gift of having my own business. I don't have the luxury of coasting through life. It's bad for my self-esteem. Whatever I'm doing is in support of what I'm passionate about. I put my purpose first, so I never feel like I'm putting myself last. And when I finish a day's work—one where I know I gave it my all—the time left for me, however much that happens to be, is that much sweeter.

Julie Castro Abrams

CEO, Women's Initiative for Self-Employment

Scrappy Kimberly says: What's the most efficient way to help ALL human beings on this planet? Help women! Help a woman and you can be pretty sure she'll help other people around her. Julie's organization has a proven ROI that would make a Fortune 500 executive green with envy—returning $30 to the local economy for every $1 invested. Where else can you invest US$1 and get thirty times your initial investment returned in taxes paid, wages increased, standard of living improved, and spirits raised? The Women's Initiative is transforming the planet for the better, one determined woman-owned business at a time. That's why I say, "Scrappy Julie Rules!"

After owning my own business and twenty years of nonprofit experience, I proudly lead Women's Initiative for Self Employment as its Chief Executive Officer. I am passionate about issues surrounding women and economic power. It is an honor to be the recipient of the Community Leader of the Year Award from Leadership California, to be named among San Francisco's "Most Influential Women," and to be recognized by the League of Women voters as a "Woman Who Could Be President." I earned my B.A. from Northwestern University and completed graduate studies in social service administration at the University of Chicago. I currently live in Novato with my husband and two beautiful children.

"Baby, you can do it, if you believe you can. If not, just fake it—it works almost as well!"
- *Anonymous*

Author

9 You Are if You SAY You ARE!

Julie Castro Abrams

I grew up in Iowa—Cedar Rapids, Iowa. I had much of the small town naïveté, but as an athlete, I also had a great drive and confidence. The combination led me to think I could do anything. So when I was too young to know anything, and too naïve to be scared, I started a business. I was twenty-two years old. What did I know? I believed I had something to offer, so other people believed it too. It worked for awhile, and the success and ultimate failure of that business has framed my life. After my own Scrappy small business failed, I decided to spend my career helping women entrepreneurs succeed. This chapter is a collection of what I learned from my own experience and their successes.

I have had the privilege of watching thousands of businesses take off. I have seen women who were square pegs in every job they ever held develop outrageously successful businesses. I have seen women who are survivors of domestic abuse create jobs for other people and be the beacon of hope for their communities. Inside every success story is a Scrappy entrepreneur, a woman who did something extraordinary where other people would have given up, and frequently many people along the way were advising her to give up! But that's not what Scrappy women do.

Here is my story.

One Day I Said, "I Am a Consultant!"...and They Believed Me

Part of my graduate program was to get an internship. During my second year, I was given an internship with the City of Chicago. I negotiated compensation as part of the internship, and was called a "consultant" for a whopping $15/hour. As I networked and met people around the city, they asked me what I did, and I explained that I was a consultant.

SCRAPPY TIP #1: Say you own a business...and you do! Business will often come to you.

People responded to my claiming to be a consultant with:

"Hey, I need a consultant. Can you set up the computer training lab for the youth center I run?"

"I need a consultant to write grants."

"I got a grant and need a consultant to work with my board."

I needed money and they needed "a consultant." I figured that, as a graduate student, if I didn't know how to do what they needed, I could learn it quickly—or I could hire someone who did. So I wrote up a brochure, got some business cards, and contracted with a few people I thought were smart, including someone to be my administrative assistant. I figured that if I had someone else to set up appointments, make calls, and manage the paperwork, I'd appear professional enough to pull this off.

Chapter 9: You Are if You SAY You ARE!

SCRAPPY TIP #2: Find out what your potential customer needs.

Although it seems like very little by today's standards, I'm a little embarrassed to admit that I eventually charged people a hefty $65 an hour as a consultant. I was only twenty-two years old when I started consulting and had very little work experience. But, boy was I confident! I was always a little shocked when people agreed to that outrageous fee. In retrospect, I believe that my relatively high fee made them take me seriously. Somehow, I instinctively knew that I had to tell them how much I charged with a straight face and not lower my price. (It doesn't work to giggle and roll your eyes when quoting your fee, or to exclaim, "Really??!!" when your client agrees to pay it.) Ladies, if you are over thirty-five you might need to go to a little therapy to be able to get through this one. For some reason, most overly educated young people have an inflated view of their own worth and value that hits a peak at about thirty, when they think everyone else must be in awe of their brilliance. After thirty-five, it seems this thing called "humility" sets in. We realize that we don't know everything, and many women start to struggle and think that somehow it means they know nothing. It really affects price-setting—thus, the anti-giggling advice.

SCRAPPY TIP #3: Be confident. Set your price and stick with it.

SCRAPPY TIP #4: The price you set impacts the "value" people perceive.

I found that I could be Scrappy and get the contract, and I could generally figure out how to add some value. But I became friends with my clients. I crossed the line. And at one point, two clients owed me a whopping $15,000. It was 1993, I was twenty-five at this point, and that was a fortune to me! They won grants from proposals I had written. But when time came to pay me, the flimsy contract I had written up wasn't enough to get me paid. And I was a wimp when faced with these experienced adults.

SCRAPPY TIP #5: Treat it like a business. Establish clear payment terms.

SCRAPPY TIP #6: Don't let business relationships become too friendly. Don't share your worries and fears with them. Stay professional!

SCRAPPY TIP #7: Have someone else act as your accountant and bookkeeper for the sake of collections. This can be your cousin Sue as long as she has a deep voice, is a little scary, and says she's your accountant.

Wow, there were a lot of tips that came out of that failure! I guess it's really true that we learn more from failure than success. Bottom line, be Scrappy when it comes to getting business but have formal business systems when it comes to getting paid.

What happened to me? I took a job with one of my clients and over the years learned a lot more about street smarts and business. I built up my list of "what I will never do when I am in charge." I learned the nuts and bolts of running a nonprofit business. And I gained a little bit of humility—but not too much! Eventually I had the opportunity to combine all of my career experience to run the Women's Initiative for Self Employment (http://www.womensinitiative.org) in San Francisco. Doesn't that sound like the best job in the world?! It is! I get to be surrounded by the smartest and most capable business leaders who want to donate their time and expertise to help Courageous (with a capital C!) women who are determined to start their own business and leave poverty. Here are a few of their stories and more Scrappy tips.

No Way Out!

Seven years after starting her successful restaurant, Cecilia says, "I can't believe what I did when I first started. I could never do that now!" When she began her business, Cecilia had no other financial options. She had to make this business work. She had been making cash wages under the table at a restaurant and really couldn't make ends meet. So she decided to branch out on her own. "When I needed to move things, I would borrow my brother's truck at four in the morning so I could get it back to him before he started work." Borrowing a truck, asking favors, working around the clock...she was being Scrappy! Putting 100 percent into her business made it possible for her to have a business that today earns her over $250K a year.

SCRAPPY TIP #8: Throw yourself into business as if you have no other options.

If you are tentative—if you consider that you might just take a full-time job if this doesn't work out—you will end up taking that job. Starting a business is a very tough challenge. It's nearly impossible if you have the temptation of full-time employment and a steady paycheck dangling in front of you. In order to hang in there through the hard times, you need to decide that there are no options other than the success of this business.

Most people have heard of *The Secret*, by Rhonda Byrne.[11] According to this book (and many similar teachings through the ages), whatever you put out there as your goal and focus on with no distractions—and no way out—that is what you will drive to accomplish. If your vision is fuzzy, or if you have an out, you will diffuse your efforts and greatly diminish your ability to succeed. I can tell you from watching scads of women breaking out of the cycle of poverty that they put every ounce of their being into their business ventures because they can't fall back on that job like I did. There is no escape clause, so they make it work.

---

11. Rhonda Byrne, *The Secret,* (Atria Books/Beyond Words, 2006).

SCRAPPY TIP #9: Ask for help. It makes other people feel good, and you need it, believe it or not.

Ladies, allow yourselves to ask for help! Women often see themselves as caretakers of everyone else and struggle to let anyone help them. But it feels great to help someone else, so don't deny others the pleasure! It is ultimately selfish if you don't allow anyone else to help you. Take my Scrappy Challenge: sit down right now and write down five things that you need to do today, and next to each one write the name of at least one person who can help you. Then, ask them. And thank them! Don't go it alone. Accept their gift of help graciously.

At 51st and Telegraph Avenue in Oakland, California, on the corner where there is no parking, and in the middle of a really rough neighborhood, stands a bakery. The bakery has no sign. (Well, actually, today it has butcher paper in the window with the handwritten name of the shop scrawled on it.) Oh, and did I fail to mention that there is a line of people out the door and around the block waiting for the scrumptious baked goods created there? Alison was making $15,000 a year selling her baked goods at the farmers' market when she started. Today she makes over $15,000 a day. How? By being Scrappy!

One day, Alison christened herself "Bakesale Betty," donned a blue wig and a 1950s outfit, and transformed into a character that is engaging and unforgettable. That was just the beginning of her journey to a multi-million dollar business. She also gives away a lot of product samples, and she remembers the names of her clients and their family members. Her husband walks down the line of waiting customers passing out warm chocolate chip cookies. They're both very generous, and always give you a little extra something when you buy a box of their popular pastries. Inside the bakery are antique ironing boards for tables and other surprising touches. Some of her customers even began blogging about her. She now has a cult-like following. Suffice it to say, Bakesale Betty has enabled Alison to take her business to a whole new level. She hasn't added a million products—she keeps it simple. She has two sandwiches, but the fried chicken sandwich is so heavenly I dream about it. (She sells 1,000 a day of that particular sandwich!)

SCRAPPY TIP #10: Be unforgettable. It doesn't have to cost a lot of money.

SCRAPPY TIP #11: Keep it simple and be the best!

SCRAPPY TIP #12: Surprise your customers...with generosity...with quality.

Will you be able to do what it takes to start your own business? Will you commit yourself to your business with complete focus? Will you believe in yourself and your value enough to ask for what you want? Will you ask for help? Will you be unique and unforgettable? If you are willing to do all of these things, my experience indicates that you will be running your own successful business someday.

After reviewing over a thousand business plans a year over many years and seeing how people fare over time, here is the great lesson I've learned. Are you ready? People who have the most academically impressive business plans almost always underperform those who have a Scrappy business plan. Not that business plans aren't important—they are. But Scrappy action beats intellectually appealing theory any day of the week.

SCRAPPY TIP #13: Don't get stuck in analysis paralysis. Plan some, then...just do it!

Knowledge Is Power, But...

Have you heard the story about how women who are elected to Congress spend their freshman nights in their hotel rooms studying every new bill so they can be experts on the content of the bill? The men, on the other hand, spend their nights networking, aligning themselves with the power brokers, asking others about the pros and cons, and getting firsthand knowledge of the perspective of key influencers. It is certainly important to be prepared. But enough already! Knowledge is power, but relationships with the right people are more powerful. Get out there and network with the power brokers. If you think you are one, and you act like one, you will become one.

SCRAPPY TIP #14: No amount of preparation and studying can match the power of networking. So go out and network!

Working in the field of microenterprise, watching women and men start businesses, I see a pattern not unlike the example of women in Congress. Men will put out a shingle, say they are in business, network, boldly ask people to invest in the business, and set aggressive goals. Ladies, I am afraid that the record shows that we gals, on the other hand:

- Don't think big enough in our business ideas, frequently confusing giving back with making money. (And we can really do both!)

- Over-prepare before taking the leap, feeling like everyone else knows something that we don't.

- Confuse requests to invest in our business with asking for help, something we think we're supposed to give, not get.

Show Me the Money!

Every business needs at least a little bit of cash to get started. If you're lucky enough to be able to fund your business startup yourself, hooray for you! But if you need money to get started, or to buy the materials to fill your first big order, keep these guidelines in mind.

When asking for investment, don't ask for money; invite people to join you.

SCRAPPY TIP #15: Remember that people want to invest in success. You need to "be" success!

People want to be part of a winning team. Show them that you're a winner and invite them to share in your success by investing. There are numerous online opportunities to solicit investment directly. There is even a website where you can put your idea out there and request a loan; then people can compete to make the loan to you by bidding with the interest they will charge you. Some people have gotten up to four rounds of funding from this source alone. You don't need five years of pro forma financial reports to get these loans! Of course, when going the conventional route, you need have all of your ducks in order.

SCRAPPY TIP #16: Show how the money will be paid back.

I know it seems obvious that investors would be interested in knowing how you plan to pay them back, but you would be surprised by how many people don't show the loan payback as part of their cash flow projections. Also, be sure to consider insurance and other important but less sexy items in your financial plans.

Oh, and don't be surprised when an interested investor asks, "How did you come up with your expected revenues?" Most revenue projects are plucked out of thin air, which doesn't make a convincing story. Show the basis of your estimate, your assumptions, the number of customers you expect to have, how that number will grow, the volumes you expect. And be sure to include your thoughts on how quickly you can grow both the supply side and the demand side. It's no use getting orders for ten thousand whatchamacallits only to find that you can't afford the raw materials, or can't ramp up production fast enough to meet that growth projection.

Unlike your own investment portfolio, past performance is often an excellent indicator of future performance. One of the most convincing ways to make your financial forecasts more believable is to find a similar business, ideally in the same area, that is willing to share their historical financial performance. If you are starting a business that typically takes three to five years to grow to a certain size, you'll be hard pressed to convince investors that you will be able to do it in a year. Investors want to see the story behind the numbers, and they want to feel confident that your numbers are realistic.

SCRAPPY TIP #17: Be bold, think big, act big, ask big, and believe in yourself.

Enough said. Just repeat Scrappy Tip #17 over and over again, and get busy!

Nathalie Udo

Scrappy Business and Life Consultant, President, InDepth Strategies, LLC

Scrappy Kimberly says: One of the reasons I adore Nathalie is that she makes me look tame by comparison—and I can't say that about a lot of people outside of the prison system! She's a motorcycle rider who looks smoking hot in leather. She's a scuba diver who goes where I sure as heck don't want to go without an endless supply of oxygen. And she's absolutely fearless in the face of many-headed demons like huge enterprise software projects and social pressures to conform. But she is one of the most reliable lunatics I know, and she is one of the few people in my life that has succeeded in getting ME to stretch MY boundaries in thinking about what's possible. Now THAT is Scrappy!

I love inspiring people to achieve what they previously thought was impossible, and have been told that my enthusiasm is infectious. I have helped my clients realize their business objectives by implementing the right amount of project management discipline, process improvement, and executive coaching, or simply through powerful project turnaround.

Don't be fooled by my girlish appearance! I have a proven record of accomplishments in leading complex international projects for corporations like the Baan Company, Boeing Corporation, Fireman's Fund, Autodesk, and Kaiser Permanente.

With my relentless energy and drive, I strive to create a lasting and positive difference through balancing structure and creativity. Having worked across many industries, continents and countries I understand the impact and importance of different cultural values and backgrounds. Believing you should live life to the fullest, wherever I can, I combine my busy work schedule with InDepth Strategies, LLC, with my two greatest passions—scuba diving and motorcycling.

"Twenty years from now you will be more disappointed by the things that you didn't do than by the ones you did do. So throw off the bowlines. Sail away from the safe harbor. Catch the trade winds in your sails. Explore. Dream. Discover."
- *Mark Twain*

Chapter

10 Don't Sweat the Downtime—Celebrate!

Nathalie Udo

Coming to the U.S.A. from Europe—the Netherlands specifically—it was a no-brainer for me to start my own business in my new home country. Being an entrepreneur in the U.S.A. is far less risky than starting a Dutch business. (Perhaps that's one of the secrets to the past economic success of the U.S.A.? It sure isn't due to easy-to-understand tax laws!) I looked into starting a consulting business back in the Netherlands, but the mountains of paperwork and stringent requirements kept me from following through with it. For starters, you need the equivalent of $125,000 in the bank to simply be able to launch your business. On top of that, there is no protection from personal liability for professional failure; any business failure will affect your personal wealth as long as you own the majority of the company. Being a small business owner means there is no way to avoid personal liability in the event of your professional demise. It would have been easier to run for political office and change the laws than to start my business, but by the time I finished investigating the options, I had no interest in either—at least in Holland.

Scrappy Geographic Lesson: There is often confusion about whether Holland is the same as the Netherlands. Even though it is printed in large letters on our export products, the usage of "Holland" is technically incorrect, as Holland is actually a region in the west-central area of the Netherlands, divided into two provinces. But bottom line, they are used interchangeably.

Here's how the whole nasty business works: if your company fails and there aren't sufficient funds available (either in the company or in your personal assets) to pay your creditors, you need to find a job. For years to come, part of your salary will be used to pay off your failed company's creditors. Now if that isn't a deterrent to entrepreneurship, I don't know what is! If you're from a place more nurturing of business startups (like just about any of the nearly two hundred countries recognized by the United Nations), you might think I'm kidding, but I'm absolutely serious.

You can imagine my surprise when I checked into starting a business in the U.S.A. I explored the different structures on the Internet, and even went to the Small Business Administration for information. When I realized that "limited liability" really means that only the money in the company is at risk, my disbelief was mind-numbing. "Are you sure?" I asked over and over again. Wow! The U.S.A. really is the land of opportunity. I started my business immediately.

Security Is an Illusion

When I first moved to the U.S.A., my well-intentioned HR manager, Ernie—a real sweetheart—did his very best to explain the concept of "at will" employment to me. It was a foreign concept to me, coming from a country where there is (or at least there was last time I checked) a two-month resignation period starting the first day of the month after you hand over your resignation letter. Let me explain: if I decide to quit my job on June 5, I am legally required to stay on the job until August 31. My conversation with Ernie went something like this: "So, you mean, if I wake up in the morning and decide that I no longer want to work here, I can just call in and quit? And that's it? I don't even have to get out of my pajamas?" "Yup!" he replied. "And it works the other way around, too. In the 'at will' system, if your manager decides there is no longer a need for you, you can be instantly shown the door." I thought this was extremely bizarre, but liberating in a way.

Once I finally understood the "at will" system, I found it confusing when my friends with "real" jobs said things like, "Oh, consulting is not for me because there are too many uncertainties." Really? Let's do some risk analysis here. (My apologies, having been a project management consultant for almost ten years, it's an occupational habit.)

I have my own health insurance, my own liability insurance, and my own pension fund, so with or without a consulting gig I am covered. True, all of this costs money, but on a monthly basis, it's not breaking the bank.

My employed friends can be laid off at any time, at which point they could be without health care, and have a lapse in pension funding. The health care issue in particular carries a very high risk if my friend happens to fall ill at the wrong time. To resolve that lack of coverage, they have some very expensive solutions that bridge gaps in coverage for people between jobs. (Or at least that's the way it works as of this writing. Who knows what will happen, as I'm writing this during the huge debate on health care reform.)

All of this seems to have the potential of being way more expensive than my monthly overhead. Maybe it's just me, but being employed sounds like a much more uncertain situation.

I'm the President!

So, off I went, starting my very own LLC—not a totally flawless process. After six months, I found out about the dreaded self-employment tax and how it would kill me financially at the end of the year. After spending too much money on a new lawyer and accountant, I managed to become an LLC that is taxed as a C corporation. Life was good!

Oh, and it just so happened that I started my business in January 2001, just like our esteemed editor, Scrappy Kimberly. Right! That was the economic downturn prior to the one in 2008–2009. Just when I decided that life was good, everything came to a standstill. No more paying work! This is the dread of every business owner or self-employed person. On top of that, I had only entered the U.S.A. at the end of 1999, and spent most of 2000 flying back and forth to Seattle managing an ERP implementation project at Boeing. This meant that I had developed no network of business connections to speak of and no local reputation, which made it tough to find work through references. Since I'm a frugal Dutch person, I had enough money in the bank to last several months. Here I was, sitting at home in my pajamas responding to job postings, checking in with my extremely thin network, but all to no avail.

One month went by. Another month went by. I kept up this internal mantra: "All is fine. I am really good at what I do, and for sure I will find my next paying gig soon!" I decided to use my downtime to strengthen my skill set by joining a few professional associations and volunteering with them in order to get myself out there among prospective clients. I have a strong dislike of networking for the sake of networking, so this was no easy matter. My Dutch heritage has ingrained in me a "do not stand out," "act normal," and "don't brag" mentality. So, even though I love to socialize, the networking felt extremely artificial and forced to me. To be honest, I hated it. But I felt that I had no choice—I had to make connections in order to keep my business alive.

The March of the Months

Around month five, I started sweating bullets. To make matters worse, I received several very interesting and tempting "real" job offers. In spite of my previous risk analysis, these offers started to seem less risky than waiting for a consulting gig as the months wore on. A real job meant real money, paid to me regularly! What to do? I am the first to admit that I'm a proud person (some say stubborn). I started my own business, and I wanted to see it through. Give up?? "No!" I thought. I couldn't give up after only a year just because of some nasty downturn in the whole economy. I'd only had one solid gig since starting my business, so throwing in the towel now was just not acceptable. "I can't give up now!" I thought, "Can I?" Nope! And I didn't. But it was tempting because....

To top it all off, my husband at the time was also cooling his heels at home, out of work. His contract got terminated about one month after mine, so you can imagine how much fun the conversations were at our home during that time. With lead in my shoes, I turned down very exciting job opportunities, resulting in sleepless nights wondering if I had done the right thing. Of course I had! Here I was, owning my own business, officially liable in a limited way, with a bit of health insurance, and with the option (if by some chance I would earn some income) to have my very own pension fund. How exciting! And scary. Onward!

Working for Nothing Pays!

Finally, after eight months (yes, eight!), I got another consulting gig based on the reputation I built while volunteering for one of the professional development associations I had joined. They reasoned that if I delivered this kind of quality work and was this driven for no money, then I would be even more excellent if they paid me. Of course, sitting on the bench for so long, aside from giving me a sore butt and depleting my finances, had also made me gun-shy. As many of you in the consulting world know, it is hard to maintain the pipeline of future business while you are actively working on a current engagement. I was determined never to be on the bench again for such a long period, so I promised myself that I'd make sure my next gig started the moment the current one ended.

Fast forward five years and it suddenly struck me that, outside of family visits to the Netherlands, I had not had a real vacation. (And I can assure you that those family visits are quite the opposite of a vacation. I desperately need a vacation after one.) Before moving to the United States, I was used to the European tradition of three to four weeks of vacation a year, which I generally spent backpacking through some part of the world. Dropping down to nothing at all was quite a shock! I had seriously neglected one of my biggest passions because I was too afraid to be without a consulting engagement again after that long dry spell.

Time to Celebrate Life

I love to travel! It gives me the opportunity to experience other cultures and meet people from around the world. I personally believe that being immersed in foreign cultures provides you with a reality check of your own perspective on life and the world around you. I have had some of the most eye-opening experiences while traveling abroad. One example that stands out was my trip to Tibet in 1998. When I left my job with KLM (Royal Dutch Airlines), I had over forty vacation days outstanding, so I was able to wave goodbye immediately after handing in my resignation and handing off to my replacement, instead of spending the mandatory two months with the company after resignation.

I used the first month off to find a new position, and spent the other traveling through Tibet. At the time, the Chinese had the tendency to close the border willy-nilly (which may still be the case), so I decided to enter from Nepal—if I wasn't allowed into Tibet, I could trek through Nepal.

The trip started with some tense moments at the border. There I was on the Nepali side with my Chinese visa and without a mandatory group visa, the group I had to travel with on the Tibetan side, and our guide in the middle trying to negotiate me over the border. The situation wasn't completely unlike a hostage negotiation. (Remind me never to get myself kidnapped!)

Somehow, I managed to slither into Tibet, and after a slight detour hiking for two hours in the middle of the night with all of our bags over a landslide of mud, snow, and ice, we were finally on our way to Lhasa.

After arriving in Lhasa, I was allowed to split from the group, so three other travelers and I hired a driver with a four-wheel-drive. Together we set off exploring the hinterlands, driving through a gorgeous landscape of two hundred different shades of brown. In the middle of nowhere on the top of a mountain we came across a nomad tent. When we got out of the car to take some pictures, the family invited us inside for some absolutely repulsive yak butter tea (very yucky!). What an experience! There I was sitting in a nomad tent sharing tea with this family in this remote region. No verbal communication was possible; however, the nonverbal message was loud and clear: pure hospitality was spoken here, even if they had barely anything to share. Looking around the tent, I visualized their life moving from pasture to pasture with their herd of yaks, carrying all of their belongings with them—truly a survival game, especially with the Tibetan winters.

It occurred to me that, even though they were living a very harsh life, it was simpler and more pure than the one I was living back home. My worries stretched from politics at work to my own personal performance, as well as loads of stuff that I thought I needed to own—none of it essential to life. I suddenly realized that the stuff I was sweating was not worth the sweat! At this moment, from this little tent with a breathtaking view of the Himalayas, I vowed to take on a new perspective on life and live it to the fullest.

Don't Sweat the Downtime!

Apparently my Himalayan perspective had gathered a bit of dust while I was working nonstop for the last five years. It was time to dust it off! I was missing out on the ability to have these amazing experiences. It was time for a change. Instead of sweating the downtime, I decided to book trips at the end of every contact, even if extension of the contract was expected. The simple reality is that if you deliver excellent work almost every company is prepared to wait two to three weeks for your return. I made this decision in 2006 and since that time I've spent two weeks in Barcelona studying Spanish and finally cashed in (or, more accurately, "cashed out") my dream dive vacation to Cocos Island off the coast of Costa Rica, diving with schools of hammerhead sharks. I've traveled to the Philippines to explore the underwater world there, and returned that same year to do my technical SCUBA dive training, plus added a week to dive the World War II wrecks of Truck Lagoon. A year later, in 2008, I explored the amazing reefs of Wakatobi in Indonesia. I owe those Himalayas a mountain of gratitude!

While I was in Indonesia, the world economy crashed. Badly!! Upon my return to the U.S., my pension fund was worth less than half of what it was when I left, and, like many of you, I was looking at a significantly later retirement than planned. With no consulting gig in hand, this felt awfully familiar. I had been here before.... Ah, right, 2001–2002. It all came back to me.

But my consulting drought was not as bad this time. I had a few small engagements—enough to pay the bills. Even though this was the worst financial downturn since the 1930s, and one of the toughest periods in my life because of some personal downturns that coincided with the global plummet, I decided to stay true to my passion. I decided that *especially* during such times I need to keep my perspective fresh, so I looked for ways to continue to explore globally during breaks in my consulting.

Since I was financially strained, I needed to be creative: use miles for the air tickets and find affordable trips. And I needed to find ways to feel like I added value, so when an email dropped into my inbox about the Thresher Shark Research & Conservation Project (TSRCP) on Monad Shoal, Malapascua Island, in the Philippines, I took a closer look. They were looking for volunteers to help with their research. The little work I had was coming to an end, and I wasn't expecting anything to materialize the last two months of 2009, so instead of sweating my downtime, and full of optimism that 2010 would be too busy to even think about a vacation, I decided to volunteer for a month.

I can tell you I have no regrets. The project focuses on collecting data to create a conservation plan for these endangered sharks. However, it also supports several families within the community (the majority of the staff being local) and, by teaching science and conservation at the local high school, equips new generations from the island with the knowledge needed to recognize and manage the issues that have such an important influence on their community. This adventure achieved exactly what I had hoped for and more: it revitalized my perspective, re-energized me, and showed me a new way to give back to the world community!

Got a break in your career? Join the club! But don't sweat it—celebrate! Take my word for it, it's worth it. Don't sweat the downtime (or small stuff either, for that matter). Take control of your life and take action!!

Sue Lebeck

Innovation Advocate

Scrappy Kimberly says: *Sue isn't the kind of woman I'd normally be drawn to right off the bat. She's pensive. She's patient. She's...relentless! And THAT is why I am inextricably woven into her adventures. She's as powerful as a stick of dynamite, and yet as gentle as a velvet glove. And she can tell you to go to hell in such a way that you'll look forward to the trip! TRULY Scrappy!*

My name is Sue Lebeck, and I'm the founder of Silicon Valley Innovation Associates, a firm focused on driving initiatives in support of innovation. Initiatives I'm leading now include "Silicon Valley Letters to Washington" and "InnovatingSMART—Celebrating SMART Innovation for a Sustainable World." For the past three years, I had the pleasure of leading the "Innovation Society" at the Silicon Valley Innovation Institute (SVII). Earlier, I founded and developed Working-Arts, a firm devoted to bringing artful perspectives to professional life. In a previous life, I spent fifteen years developing collaborative networking software and standards, predecessors to the tools I rely upon today.

My work is inspired and informed by my background in the sciences and the arts. I have a graduate degree in computer science, and another in clinical psychology and creative expression. In my varied career, I enjoyed fifteen years in networking software design and development, technology leadership, and program management, then five years in expressive arts program development, education and counseling, and most recently, five years supporting creativity and innovation in the workplace and beyond.

A program director and former software architect, I understand the power of well-designed frameworks and procedures to build and evolve effective systems. A creativity teacher and innovation advocate, I also understand the human processes of creativity and innovation, and the elements needed to foster it.

"The Constitution only gives people the right to pursue happiness. You have to catch it yourself."
- Benjamin Franklin

---

11 Grace and the Artful Professional

Sue Lebeck

My professional story has taken me from one extreme to the other—from an uber-left-brain career to an uber-right-brain one—and back again to center. Looking back, I see that my whole brain has been at work all along, bringing first a human emotionality to the computer world, and later a software engineer's logic to the emotional world. I ultimately found myself in the unofficial but artful profession of "innovation advocacy," a role I have naturally played all along.

In my story, I am accompanied by a very Scrappy ally, a Princess of Good Fortune. I call her "Grace." Grace sometimes appears in the recognizable forms of health, wealth, love, and success. At other times, she comes disguised as pain, sorrow, loss, and confusion. Always, she is my friend. I hope that my story tugs at yours, and reveals the presence of Grace at work in your life, too.

Scrappy Story, Full of Grace

When I was young, I was a strong student of math and science, but could in no way picture myself working in a lab or a hospital. Squeamish and klutzy, I could only imagine myself in an office, "being helpful in some way." Secretary, I guess! This limited aspiration was not cool with my advisors and teachers, or with my very Scrappy mother, or even with me. But what other career was there for a klutzy science girl? Enter the new field of "computer science," a mysterious subject one of my female cousins had taken up. Math? Check. Science? Check. Office? Check! Knowing nothing else about this emerging field, Grace gave me a decision and a future. It was 1977.

In college, at a progressive Catholic university named Clarke, I learned to program computers using punched cards. Clumsily modern, this process taught me to think carefully and get things right the first time, as the opportunity for programming experiments came at a rate of only one chance per day! (Imagine forgetting an "end-if" and having it slip your schedule by twenty-four hours!) Thoroughness of thought continues to be a gift, though a sometimes pesky, obstacle to my more creative side.

My first computer job came to me through a tried and true method—an introduction by my mother. I was frightened to begin my first serious job, but my mother insisted, "Just pretend you can, until you can." This proved to be excellent advice! In fact, I've learned, it is how all creative acts are accomplished.

After college, I went to the University of Wisconsin because the department chair at my small Iowa college *made* me. Of course, I put up a fight! I had a great job offer from IBM, and I felt really "done" with school. But my department chair was a very Scrappy nun. She was the first woman in the world to earn a Ph.D. in computer science—you can never tell about nuns by looking at them—and she saw potential in me. She persisted, and I compromised: I would go, but only if the university gave me a teaching assistantship. I got my TA-ship—and an office to boot. I called my nearly new boss at IBM to apologize. He wished me well, and Grace went with me off to Madison.

Graduate school was an eye-opener. I had always been near the top of my classes before, but now I found myself playing with some (seemingly) bigger boys. After a bout of depression, and bolstered by sheer stubbornness and pride, Grace pulled me through this initial tough spot and helped me find my stride as a strong student again. Along the way I got to teach—the most fulfilling challenge of all.

Master's degree in hand, I was hired by the university into a corporate-funded networking applied research project (quite a mouthful). Now, I knew nothing at all about networking, but so what? Neither did anyone else! It was simply too new a field to be crammed with experienced professionals. In spite of our lack of prior experience, here we were, putting some alphabet soup called "TCP/IP" onto an IBM machine for the first time, and connecting the IBM internal email network to the formerly military-only ARPAnet. It was 1983. This was radical!

From that point on, networking became the science and the art of my life. Computer networking was the *platform*, but networking *people* was the point.

In the midst of this professional stroke of luck, I married my grad school sweetheart, a gifted software guy who eventually begged me to move to Silicon Valley to follow his dream. Reluctant to follow the super-geek pack to California (too predictable!), I nevertheless succumbed for love. Leaving behind my university research job, my many volunteer projects, and my imminent plans for motherhood, we drove west over the mountains, with REM's "It's the end of the world as we know it, and I feel fine!" on endless repeat. It was 1989.

In Silicon Valley, Tandem Computers and I embraced each other, and I began my career as a technology manager. Ostensibly, I guided network software development projects and helped facilitate the development of new and improved networking standards. Actually, I was there to empathize with people through their triumphs and frustrations, help get things in line when things got out of whack, and enjoy frequent, informal opportunities to teach.

I had the good fortune to work with some very creative people. A keenly perceptive and progressive manager told me I had a well-developed connection between my "left" and "right" brain. It was a new concept to me, and apparently somewhat uncommon in the computer engineering world. He appreciated my ability to bridge the technical and human sides of work. Indeed, this was the real work I had embarked upon when Grace found me my math-and-science office career. As intended, I was really there primarily to "be helpful in some way."

Two years into my seven years at Tandem, Grace finally allowed me to have my baby. A delightfully artistic little girl, my daughter would later make possible my introduction to the artful course-change of my life.

Endings and Beginnings

I should have seen it coming. Mere months after moving to California, the Loma Prieta earthquake gave my personal and professional foundations a shake. Seven years later, a series of events rocked my world completely, in painful yet transformational ways. Accustomed to a great job, a happy family, and a comfortable life, I expected to enjoy only more of the same. Instead, in 1996 my world really did come to an end as I knew it. I was challenged by Grace and circumstance to forget all that I knew and begin, creatively, again.

The World Wide Web had hit corporate America. While the information architect in me was elated, the web turned my messaging industry into a commodity, and much of my future-leaning work become instantly irrelevant. Similarly disrupted, my company was in existential crisis. A fault-tolerant computing giant, computing advances had radically changed its market, and its inevitable future was strategically disconnected from its successful past. Even my marriage, until then the anchor of my life, began to crack at the seams.

In response to this culmination of crises, my inner "white knight" rose up and tried futilely to make everything okay. He failed in every dimension. My husband and I separated. I positioned myself for layoff and prayed to be let go. Grace obliged.

De-horsed, depressed, demoralized, and deeply relieved, I stepped away from life as I knew it. I sought to rebuild my world quickly. I immediately re-partnered, and once my severance ran out, I made an effort to get back on the horse again and find my place in the world that was once my expert domain. Though offered several promising positions, in the end a little bird whispered in my ear to stop me. "No," it said, "this is not where you belong." Perhaps, but now what?

My former husband reminded me that his company had recently gone public, a highly successful move that had left us both suddenly wealthy. At least for the time being, I didn't actually have to work. But who was I if I wasn't working? Did I even exist? Born and bred with a midwestern work ethic, I was devastated. Not work? Why, what use would I be then? This was the most liberating and most frightening moment of my life. Financial cushion in place, I allowed myself to fall....

Reluctantly Embracing an Artful Life

Motherhood broke my fall, just in time for my almost-five-year-old daughter and me. Underserved by her workaholic mother up till now, my girl gave me a new focus, a clear purpose, a steady joy, and many outlets for my penchant for volunteer work. The "Art Docent" volunteer teachers program in my daughter's school district introduced me to a truly foreign medium. (Computer scientists aren't required to take a lot of art classes—OK, make that ANY.) Thus, Grace nudged me forward, and I dipped my toe into developing what Carl Jung would call my inferior functions. I was now lurching fitfully forward toward art, both as teacher and student, and toward a new focus for my life.

I enjoyed motherhood, personal freedom, volunteering, outdoor hikes, and elementary art lessons for a glorious year. Still, bliss was not mine, because all the while I was not-so-secretly fretting for my professional future. My identity was still very entangled with my work, and I was uneasy with my otherwise fortunate story.

As I tossed about at psychic sea, another little bird spoke to me. This one came disguised as a jeweler with an interest in transpersonal psychology. What in the world is transpersonal psychology? I didn't have a clue. As it happens, I had always wanted to study psychology, and had even checked it out with the career center service that had come with my severance. On the psychology shelf, next to the dated binders indicating that my financial future would be dismal, was a book titled *So You Want to Be a Therapist* by Patricia F. Ross. Inside was a list of ten personal "issues" that you must not have if you were to contemplate this treacherous path. I had eight. "Better stick to computers," I thought.

But "transpersonal psychology!" Now, this seemed like something else altogether. TP, a school of psychology that traveled beyond mere humanism and dared to include the (say it in a whisper) *spiritual*, was just what I needed. I truly believe that, at some point in our lives, TP may be what everyone needs—especially at that dastardly mid-point, that crisis point we all hit that shocks us out of our egos and into something beyond. Being in crisis and duly shocked, I was ready to listen.

Thanking Grace, I joined a wonder-full cohort at the Institute of Transpersonal Psychology in Palo Alto, California, and began a journey of self-discovery and healing. My time at ITP provided me with a clinical degree, a unique opportunity to teach, exquisite mentors, and a surprising fascination and respect for the power of the arts and the creative process.

My work at ITP taught me much about the tender and vulnerable process that is creativity. The creative process is a "North Star" vision—clear and beckoning, yet incredibly vague. It is driven by curiosity, intuition, and persistence. It is infused with paradox—knowing and not-knowing, triumph and humility, personal authority and complete surrender. It is dynamic, filled with frustration, elation, confusion, and discovery. It is a collaboration with the divine. The big *"Aha!"*—Life is a creative process.

The Artful Professional

After ITP, I practiced a few years as an expressive arts therapist and teacher, a fascinating role, which I very much enjoyed. In this role, I was able to help people move through difficult material, and unleash insight, energy, and healing. But before long, I had to answer the loud and nagging call to return to my originally chosen place of work. I still wanted to "be helpful in some way" in the corporate office.

This time Grace led me to create Working-Arts, a practice designed to bring the power of the arts to the workplace. Working-Arts is grounded in three art forms that pervade our lives: image, character, and story. Image speaks to our intuition, and helps us see what our right brain knows. Story, the driver of all that we do, shapes the very plot line of our seemingly objective choices. And character de-personalizes our conflicting positions, allowing our humanity to see what's possible. Through the conscious application of these three forms, workplace challenges can be understood, and people can be inspired and energized—even transformed.

Unfortunately for Working-Arts, the Internet bubble-burst of 2001 had just occurred. The workplace was cutting costs ruthlessly and dropping its support for human arts everywhere but marketing. Post-boom-and-bust, the organizational development (OD) community—my most understanding ally in getting work in the corporate world—was often denied opportunities to do its own important work. Nevertheless, Working-Arts refused to die. It developed a very small and appreciative client base, and a newsletter to share the iceberg-tip of its ideas. "The Artful Professional" enjoyed a modest but loyal set of readers for the next couple of years.

Grace next led me next to a rare opportunity to study as a teacher-in-training with the Creativity in Business (CIB) program of Stanford fame. This program grounded transpersonal principals in business-appropriate heuristics. With CIB, the potent and vulnerable creative process was gently nudged open with four fundamental practices:

1. have no expectations,
2. turn off the "Voice of Judgment,"
3. see precisely, and
4. ask dumb questions.

This is a potent model, and an infinite number of additional heuristics can be built atop these four. Armed with my CIB tools, and inspired by a gifted teaching team and cohort, I connected with the archetypal and challenging "Hero's Journey" we were each embarking on.

From Creativity to Innovation

At this time, Grace led me to my next important insight: creativity was an expressive doorway, but innovation was the key to unlocking the far-reaching *value* of creativity. In other words, for creativity to become valuable it had to be invited, shaped, and used in ways that many people could benefit from. To capture what I had learned in a way that made it easier to share with others, I developed an "innovation architecture"—a model for turning raw creativity into successful innovation. This architecture, unlike the software architectural drawings of my earlier days, was a series of concentric circles. At the center of these circles was the creative and widespread "source." At the outer edge was "celebration," to be applied to even the smallest achievement of innovation success. Key innovation-coaxing elements lay in between: infrastructure (to manage and make space for creativity), invitation (to inspire and make safe the creative process), evaluation (applied carefully and not too soon, so as not to kill great ideas in their infancy), and execution (an experimental and ongoing creative process). Later, I learned to add "collaboration," without which very little value-creation occurs.

My ideas matured, and I was chomping at the bit to find a forum for unleashing them. As a first step, Grace sent something wonderful and painfully confusing my way.

I was on a weeklong arts facilitation gig with a collaborative group called Dreamfish, and was hit by an archetypal event that psychologists call an "animus reaction." Specifically, I fell madly in love with a man who seemed to be my Knight in Shining Armor. (Has this ever happened to you? I felt like I had glimpsed heaven, and that I would now live happily ever after.)

Carl Jung's teachings explain much about life, and this is no different. Jung suggests that very often when we fall in love with someone it is because we have caught a glimpse of our own inner "other." Our own unrealized self-image is reflected back in the look, behavior, talent, and aspiration of our love-ee. This guy was everything I was looking for—poised, artistic, a save-the-world guy, a respected social systems leader. But splat! My dream ended as quickly as it began, leaving me dazed, confused, and writhing in pain. Ouch!

Finally, I realized I might never have really been in love with *him*. I was in love with what he was—what I wanted to be! I *had* glimpsed heaven and happiness *was* within reach. But this was for me to create—not someone else.

Well, this is easy to say now, but it took six months, a "Jewel" CD played repeatedly, and a great deal of expressive art-making to sort this out. Grace was with me the whole way, and together, sort it out we did. I emerged realizing that I was the poised, artistic, social and systems-oriented leader that I first saw in someone else. Thank you, Grace!

Close-to-whole at last, I was ready to get on with my life. No longer looking for my self in someone else, my real-life love relationship could finally relax into its true potential. Within a few years, I would be happily married again. Meanwhile, a launching platform for my innovation work extended towards me like a bridge to my next adventure.

This launching platform was SVII—the Silicon Valley Innovation Institute. An innovation management educational nonprofit, SVII allowed me a lot of room for experimentation. Among these experiments, I had the opportunity to lead a rich community of what we came to call "innovation advocates." These self-identifying "creatives" periodically come together from unseen corners and every field to share stories, metaphors, perspectives, challenges, lessons, and community dinners. My role at SVII led me to seek out stories and players in the vast and often unsung dimensions of our innovation community here in Silicon Valley, a location known for creative genius which is sometimes rewarded, frequently discouraged, and often punished. I became intensely interested in the "Hero's Journey" of innovation, and began to seek new ways to support innovative people, innovation leaders and the evolving innovation community. I launched an informal community of leaders, collaboratively developed a set of potential innovation-supporting initiatives, and geared up for an expanded adventure in innovation advocacy.

New Beginnings

But Grace sent me another unexpected gift. Interrupting my momentum, she sent me on a surprise journey through breast cancer. ("Gee, do I have time for that now, Grace?! I'm kinda busy here!") Luckily, at the time I was literally filled with Grace, as I had recently returned from a girlfriend pilgrimage to Elvis' "Graceland." Through the gift of early detection, an existential crisis was averted and a valuable opportunity was created. My diagnosis landed me on a powerful path, a path to help me reconstruct—physically and metaphorically—the shields on my heart. The next months brought a greatly slowed pace, a focus on my self, and much sweetness. My health challenge gifted me with sweet support from my newlywed husband, sweet art-filled time with my painterly daughter, and sweet rest and think time. Reduced and rebuilt (quite literally), I emerged from my downtime ready to explore and bring focus to the most potent possibilities on my collaborative doorstep.

Lurching forward again with Grace, I have since started a new business and launched several collaborative initiatives in the service of evolving innovation. This latest Hero's Journey will be aided by many gifted allies who have often personified Grace to me. The journey will require me to be very Scrappy, and very artful, to be sure. I can't wait to begin!

There is no map for the Hero's Journey—every one of us must walk her own unique path. But here are a few guidelines I've collected during my own adventure that I hope will light your way, and a poem to light your heart. Although the road seems at times to wind uphill all the way, it's a journey I wouldn't have missed!

Scrappy Practices

- Pretend you can, until you can.
- Listen to those who see your potential.
- Say "yes" when you can. Say "no" when you must.
- Always believe in yourself.

- During a "fall," be gentle with yourself, and listen carefully.

- As you get older, begin to embrace your "inferior functions."

- Study with great teachers whenever you can.

- Celebrate every success, however small.

- When you fall in love, ask yourself, who does this person represent in me?

- Embrace "downtime" that comes your way. Create some from time to time.

- If stuck, change your structure. This will allow something new to happen.

- During times of struggle, create a credible and inspiring story that will keep you going. Make it up out of thin air if you have to!

- Every Hero's Journey depends on allies to achieve success. Be always on the lookout for well-aligned and trustworthy allies. Be always on the lookout to *be* a well-aligned and trustworthy ally.

Artful Practices

- Recognize Grace when she appears, even if she's wearing one of her unattractive disguises.

- Do not fear the unknown.

- Embrace what insists on emerging.

- Be thoughtful, forward-thinking, and prepared. Then, surrender and improvise.

- Listen to "little birds."

- When destruction is all around, be creative.

- Don't miss your opportunity to relish the children in your life.

- If real life isn't making sense, look for the archetype or metaphor—much may be revealed.

- Whatever you do, notice what you are *really* doing.

- Notice any story you may inadvertently find yourself in, and discover what character you are playing. Play it graciously, or seek a new role for yourself.

Artful Practices from "The Artful Professional"

- Story drives our every experience. Know what story you are living, and transform it if necessary.

- When in conflict, identify the points of view, or "characters" at play. De-couple them from the people who speak for them. Focus in turn on each character and come to know what they see, think, feel and need. Once the characters are understood, the conflict will often resolve itself quickly.

- Surround yourself with art images and objects that inspire you. Change them as your needs and activities change.

- "Ask Art"—When you have a question or challenge, look to art imagery for inspiration. Choose images that call to you, and write down precisely what you see. Then read your writing out loud, as though it were a poem. A poetic view will help you see the deeper meanings that are present.

If you would like to seed an art imagery collection, contact me at my Working-Arts persona, sue@working-arts.com. I will send you a starter kit from my pathologically vast collection. My husband will be so happy to be rid of some of this enormous pile!

Finally, a recent poem from my own "Ask Art" practice:

The Essentials of Life

Beautiful, modern—
we can grow something new,
much like before.

There is wisdom in these minds
which come together now.
We are what we create.

We keep what we love
close to our skin.
What do we love?

Trust in lucky pennies.
Hearts and minds do impossible things.

Embrace the generations.
And dance with heightened joy.

Bend when you can, burn when you must,
bounce when you are thrown.

These are the essentials of life.

Wrap Up—You Can Be Ubuntu, Too!

"Life has taught us that love does not consist in gazing at each other, but in looking outward together in the same direction."
- *Antoine de Saint Exupery*

All my life I've craved a meaningful connection with what I can only describe as "my kind." At last I have found them! They're nestled in the pages of this book and roaming the halls of the business world globally. Perhaps you've felt the same yearning for connection, and maybe even glimpsed it as you read. Although some of us have the luxury of living as if we are independent of other people, the truth is that we are all interconnected and interdependent. I strongly believe that authentically sharing our stories is the first step in dissolving the illusion of separateness, bridging us through our shared human experience. This concept is captured in the Bantu word "ubuntu," which I recently encountered on my quest to discover ways of building community. It's time for Scrappy Businesswomen everywhere to embrace ubuntu!

Ubuntu is a word originating in southern Africa, like one of our authors, Eldette. It expresses our deep interconnectedness and interdependence, and I find this concept the perfect note on which to close our time together here. In his 2004 book

God Has a Dream, Archbishop Desmond Tutu explained what it meant to be a person with ubuntu: "Such people are open and available to others, wiling to be vulnerable, affirming of others, do not feel threatened that others are able and good, for they have a proper self-assurance that comes from knowing that they belong in a greater whole." This is the kind of spirit that I feel rising in me as I read the stories in this book. At various time throughout my life people have cautioned me about how women in the business world are competitive and spiteful to each other. I've been fortunate not to experience much of that in my career, and I refuse to fall into the trap of searching for confirming evidence. Sure, there are plenty of examples of people acting like jerks at work, but I haven't gathered any statistically meaningful evidence that suggests that it gets doled out according to gender. Scrappy Women in Business certainly feel no need to tear each other down. They know that they are connected to each other. They draw strength from each other. They encourage each other. They help each other, and they even celebrate each others' successes, knowing that one person's victory does not require another's defeat.

A few years after publishing his book, Archbishop Tutu expanded on his explanation of ubuntu by adding, "Ubuntu speaks particularly about the fact that you can't exist as a human being in isolation.... You can't be human all by yourself, and when you have this quality—Ubuntu—you are known for your generosity. We think of ourselves far too frequently as just individuals, separated from one another, whereas you are connected and what you do affects the whole world. When you do well, it spreads out; it is for the whole of humanity."[12]

We truly *are* in this together, and once we "get" that we have an entirely different relationship with the people around us in the business world, both men and women. Suddenly we can focus on making the pie bigger instead of arguing over who gets the crumbs. We can start seeing possibilities that we were previously blind to. Perhaps most importantly, we can start asking for and offering help. When we perceive other people as connected to ourselves, it makes no sense to behave otherwise. Generosity is a natural consequence of interdependence.

---

12. http://en.wikipedia.org/wiki/Ubuntu_(philosophy)

Being a Scrappy Woman in Business is not something I'd attempt alone in a million years! We need each other. Let's stick together.

How Will You Be Remembered?

At the moment I can't imagine retiring. Maybe it's just an overabundance of adrenaline coursing through my veins as a result of meeting my last five deadlines by working furiously throughout the night, but I have a hard time visualizing myself finding fulfilment through an endless stream of gardening, travel, and leisure. I've also noticed that retirement frequently precedes death. Although this doesn't prove retirement causes death, I'm not taking any chances. To be honest, I think I'm addicted to work. And like many people, I have an incentive to stay addicted—my monthly credit card bill and a mortgage the size of the GDP of a small country.

In spite of my aversion to retirement, I'd like you to imagine your own retirement party. What do you want people to be saying about you at this celebration as they all look back on your career? How do you want your colleagues to remember you? Here are a few phrases that I hope never to hear at my own retirement celebration, should I ever find myself at such an unlikely event:

"She was always polite and well-behaved."

"She was extremely agreeable and easy to get along with."

"She was completely inoffensive in every way."

By now you can guess that there's very little chance that anyone would say any of these things, and if they did the result would be bursts of uncontrollable laughter from the entire crowd. No, I don't intend to be remembered this way, and if you want to be a Scrappy Woman in Business, neither should you. When you retire, I hope people wax on about your indomitable spirit, your feisty determination, your hair-raising courage, and your inexhaustible sense of humor. I hope they ramble on incessantly about how you inspired them with your persistence and ingenuity, and how you eschewed the easy path in favor of one that was more true to yourself. I hope they endlessly praise the generosity with which you reached out to others to help them achieve their goals. Finally, I hope you can honestly say that you have no regrets—that no stone was left unturned, that no worthy challenge was left unexplored, that no dream was left rotting by the side of the road.

Don't despair if the complexion of your career has a few blemishes and pock marks. There's makeup for that. When we compare ourselves to others we are standing in an unflattering light. From the outside, success often looks easier than it is. Chances are that the person you admire (or feel intimidated by) has just as much debris in their past as you do. Discouraged sometimes? It happens! Make mistakes now and then? We've all made doosies! Daunted by the challenges you face? That's a sign that you're facing challenges worthy of you! Afraid you're not up to it? Only the most arrogant among us escape these kinds of doubts. Lurch forward nonetheless.

The Scrappy Goddess comes bearing the gifts of reward and challenge in the same hand, leaving the other free to reach out to catch you when you fall. You must accept both gifts together, trusting that the other hand will support you when you need it—usually in the form of some other Scrappy Businesswoman, sometimes from where you least expect it.

So Now You Know

So now you know. At some level, there is only one of us. Don't be fooled into thinking you are any less capable than others based on the thin veneer that separates us from one another. Don't give up just because of one—or many—setbacks. Don't settle for anything less than what you are capable of. Don't listen to the voices that undermine your strengths, especially those inside your own head. You are a Scrappy Businesswoman! You are travelling with a tribe of other such women on a journey to what's possible.

Personally, I'm determined to live my life with no regrets. Life's biggest regrets are the result of ignoring our intuition about who we are and what we are capable of, only to look back years later and wistfully think "If only..." When you look back, I hope you will shout, "Wooo hooo!"

All of us Scrappy Women in Business celebrate your spirit, and encourage you to continue boldly on your journey—unapologetic for your strength and graciously proud of your awesome power. And as you climb the ladder of business success, remember to reach back and lend a hand to those following behind you.

- Scrappy Kimberly

"Never stand begging for that which you have the power to earn."
- *Miguel de Cervantes*

Other Happy About Books

Scrappy Project Management®

This book is for people who need to get things done...especially project managers.

Paperback $19.95
eBook $14.95

Scrappy General Management

This book will provide you with the 7 common sense and repeatable steps that will guide you through running a business that everyone will be proud to be associated with.

Paperback:$19.95
eBook: $14.95

***#LEADERSHIPtweet
Book01***

This book outlines a framework and a mechanism for both learning new things and applying current knowledge in a thoughtful and practical way.

Paperback $19.95
eBook $14.95

42 Rules for Working Moms

This book assembles the guidance of contributors from all over the world who offer their thoughts on topics ranging from raising polite children and making time for yourself, as well as your mate, to losing the mommy guilt and delegating at home.

Paperback $19.95
eBook $14.95

Purchase these books at Happy About
http://happyabout.info
or at other online and physical bookstores.

Breinigsville, PA USA
22 August 2010
243986BV00007B/2/P